SUFISM
FOR TODAY

Omar Ali-Shah

alif

Edited by Augy Hayter from tape recordings

Copyright © by Tractus Books, Paris

ISBN 2 - 909347 - 00 - 1

alif
Alif Publishing Corporation
P.O.Box 507
FDR Station
New York, N.Y. 10150-0507
&
Tractus Books, Paris
43 rue de la Gaïté
75014 -Paris
France

CONTENTS

The Sufi Tradition

The Sufi Tradition is not a religion, nor is it a cult. It is a philosophy of life, and its purpose is to offer to man a practical path to enable him to achieve a measure of higher consciousness, (and) through this elevated consciousness, to be able to understand his relationship with the Supreme Being.

This philosophy has been handed down through the ages. It has retained the ancient quality and has guarded its ancient secrets so that it may be available, unchanged and untarnished, to those who seek deeper wisdom through deeper consciousness.

The Tradition holds that man, in his present state, is a conditioned being : conditioned from birth to accept, more often than not, without care or reference, a multitude of attitudes, points of reference and theories that bind his thoughts and actions throughout life. This conditioning is not all bad or negative, and some is necessary. Faith, piety, discipline, trust, obedience and order are all qualities that are noble and should be taught, learnt and practised.

We hold that the purity of man's inner being, in harmony with the Scheme of the Master Designer, can lift him from the mundane and shield him from the corruption and contamination of the "world outside". This does not mean a need to retreat into a mountain cave or hermitage. On the contrary, it means to be a full (and) better member of society; to be "in the World and not of the World"; to follow rules and disciplines to bring an inner peace, and by example, to instruct other worthy people, with humility and purpose; to hark to

i

the voice of Nature that the secrets of the Tradition may become known, but only to those whose intentions are pure, (and who) can swear, Witnessed be the Lord of Life, that they will use the Wisdoms truly and well.

From the earliest days, the saying Ex Oriente Lux has inspired many Saints and sages to seek the chord of harmony that would link East to West to mutual benefit. Saint Francis of Assisi debated with Arabian and Khorassani sages, Ignatius Loyola corresponded with Masters of the Tradition, the Emperor Frederick the Great had an Arab advisor. During the unfortunate period of the Crusades, Templars and Hospitalers held secret conclave to prevent tragic excesses on both sides.

It is a fact of history that in the Tradition, the checkerboard pavement is a feature of certain "tekkias" or "places of assembly and power" : in these cases, black, representing both wisdom and toil, and white, representing joy and the Morning Star.

A worthy person, entering the Tradition, must do so freely (and) not as the result of inducements or promises. He is bound by an oath to seek deep knowledge and a permanent consciousness, that he may progress, and by doing so, uplift his fellow men.

A teacher in the Tradition is a person who has undergone highly precise training in both his inward and outward (or worldly) life. His mandate to teach will come from an unimpeachable source of authority, and at all times and for all his actions, he will answer to the Great Designer.

The Sufi Tradition is in no way incompatible with everyday life and laudable activities within the community. Certainly the aim of each Sufi is to develop a greater inward awareness of our Divine Creator; and through approaching this knowledge, bestow good upon himself, his near and dear, and his community. At no time should his adherence to the Sufi path bring him into conflict with the powers of Nature, nor suppress his deep conscience.

The Tradition is offered to the West with sincerity and deep purpose. If the Sufi message finds an echo in the West, then let its fraternity transcend time and distance, and may the sharing of the Secrets bring this planet into Divine Favour.

Omar Ali-Shah

Thirty Years On

The story, as far as the disciples are concerned, really begins around 1960, with a number of people in London and Paris who had been in contact with Ouspensky's teaching groups and later directly with Gurdjieff, Ouspensky's original mentor.

Some description of the context in London and Paris before the arrival of the Shah brothers is necessary. Without trying to fight ancient battles anew, it has to be said that Gurdjieff's death in 1949 left a very messy heritage, with many different people trying to carry on his work. Jeanne de Salzmann, one of his early disciples, eventually imposed a measure of "order" on the various activities and succeeded in institutionalizing the so-called "Gurdjieffian" teaching. Her authority was accepted by many of Gurdjieff's followers, but by no means all of them: she was able to set up an organized hierarchy under her leadership which still exists today with her son Michel de Salzmann in charge.

A large number of people, who had been connected with "Gurdjieffian" activities, in Paris and London would not go along with this so-called succession in the fifties, and were on the lookout for a properly mandated exemplar of the ancient teaching, because even if they only had counterfeit coin in their hands, they realized that the true gold did exist.

Throughout this period in Paris, a woman called Vera Page, who was the widow of the poet Rene Daumal and later the wife of the British Landscape Architect Russel Page, had refused to submit to the rule of Mme. de Salzmann, and had organized a group based on

Gurdjieffian ideas. She had known Gurdjieff and her teaching was strongly influenced by him. There were therefore two parallel activities going on in London and Paris, supported by some older members with considerable experience, most of whom had personally known Gurdjieff.

Vera Page came down with cancer in 1961 and died soon after. The future of the Paris group became a matter of great concern, all the more so since some of the younger people began manifesting a desire to take things over, which was something the older members were wise enough not to desire.

It was at about this time that Reginald Hoare read a travel article about Afghanistan in Blackwood's Magazine: in this article there was a description of a Sufi exercise that was known only to the top ten ranked Gurdjieffians of the period. Reggie thought that behind the pseudonym of the author there had to be someone who knew a great deal about the Tradition and where it came from, and Reggie wrote a letter to the author care of the Editor in order to make contact with him.

Idries Shah, who later described that article as "trawling", replied to this letter as author of the article. Reggie met him, became convinced of introducing him to various ex-Gurdjieffians in England and France. Shah agreed to teach some of them, and rejected others.

Although Russel Page was under considerable pressure to take on the leadership of the Paris group himself, to his great credit he asked Shah to take charge of this seriously drifting group, and Shah accepted. The first meeting between Shah and the Paris group took place in spring 1962. Omar Ali-Shah or "Agha" as we came to call him, was still traveling at this time: he appeared on the scene a while later.

Our instructions were to write a personal letter saying why one was in the group, to cease reading any of Gurdjieff's writings immediately, and to stop practicing the movements (an example of these somewhat robotic stylized movements can be seen at the end of the film MEETINGS WITH REMARKABLE MEN; the people on screen are mostly adepts from that time).

In 62 and 63, most of the activities centered on England: there were three day meetings at Coombe Springs, a place that had been made over to Idries Shah by John Bennett.

Thursday exercises in Paris started with listening to the OM MANE PADME OM mantra, followed by tapes of Shah reading Sufi texts. The Lataif came later. At a meeting in England, Shah announced that his brother would come and live among us in Paris.

The publication of THE TEACHERS OF GURDJIEFF by Rafael Lefort in 1966 completed the breakup with the institutionalized successors of Gurdjieff, because the origin of Gurdjieff's teaching (which he always vague about) and its limitations due to Gurdjieff's own personality are very clear in this book. The one idea that was and is unbearable to Gurdjieff's followers is that he was simply one of many people who passed through the hands of the Khwajagan or Central Asian School of Naqshbandi Sufis: the book attracted criticism for being cast in fable form, and it was also said that Gurdjieff's teachers would no longer have been alive to talk about it in the sixties. But in so far as there in no indication that the events recounted in the book took place at this time, the argument doesn't hold water: how can you criticize a book both for being a fable and for being inaccurate on dates?

Agha came to live with us in 63/64. Many non-esoteric activities were launched at this time: a space was rented and sales were organized in order to raise money. It was necessary at this time to decompress from the strongly esoteric orientation of the Gurdjieffians. People talked a lot, and one sees now that Agha was disconnecting people from overtly "esoteric" thinking, inducing all of us to think about things more simply. People were asked to bring along their esoteric literature for inspection: most of it ended up sold off to second-hand booksellers. Once again: this operation must be seen in context. To my knowledge Agha has never censored anybody's reading matter since, and would not think of doing so.

Right from the beginning Agha always said he was a "traditionalist"; we were always ready to believe him, but most of us had no idea what this meant. The organization of camping and other trips together is an example of an adaptation of an old technique which Agha recycled for modern times. Caravans and the pilgrimage to Mecca were means of providing novel common experiences and refining the contact between dervishes in the old days: it is probably fair to say that our own caravans and gatherings fulfill the same function.

We had an old antique store that became the Tradition shop after the group had put a considerable amount of labor into it. I came along in the autumn of 64 to help with the plastering, was very taken with Catherine, who began to explain to me what was going on. It was kind of mystifying: whatever these people were together, they certainly were not exactly pals. We scraped and painted walls with great energy and enthusiasm: nobody really knew how to do any of these jobs.

Personal story: the night before the opening of the boutique was a Thursday. While others did the exercise, I went on working to prepare the shop, which was absolutely filthy for the vernissage. Instead of joining us to help clear up after the exercise, most of the group went off to a restaurant nearby to have dinner leaving only a few of us to finish off. Agha and his wife passed by on their way to join the others, and Agha immediately took in the situation, rolled up his sleeves and began cleaning by our side.

He had a highly personal style with the broom and dustpan. He would sweep up all the junk and garbage into a pile right in the middle of the shop, and then go off to look for the dustpan, tracking everything he had swept back over the floor. He would then find the dustpan, bring it back into the middle whereupon he would have mislaid the broom somewhere, so that he had to put the dustpan down somewhere else and go looking for the broom. He would then carefully sweep everything back into the center of the shop, and the whole process would begin again.

This went on, very meticulously, several times over: by the end we were all just looking at Agha with our mouths agape. He was going through this frenetic activity without cracking a smile, like Buster Keaton. Suddenly something occurred to me: Agha was us. He was in fact incarnating everything I had seen going on over the past three months: Bella pouring nitric acid on the tiles in order to clean them and reacting indignantly when we screamed at her after it dripped on us from above; Jean-Pierre stripping away the plaster so efficiently that he broke through the wall into the next building, etc. But what was strange and somehow impressive was that he was playing us without guying us, without being superior; he was serious, convinced, and totally inefficient. What I realized in that moment, which changed my life, was that he was not only showing us where we were, but he was doing it from where we were, at that time, and not from above.

ix

Now we all have things in our life we did wrong
and things we did right: my own "quiet pride" is that
with not so much to go on, I recognized my teacher. It
could of course be put in another way: my teacher did
me the honor of allowing himself to be recognized by
me. After my father died quite recently, I further
realized that it was his own example as a teacher of
print making that had enabled me to evaluate what a
real teacher is.

It is very difficult to put across our lack of
awareness at that time. We had no idea of a Master's
status, and Agha never talked to us about how we
should treat him, or use him: he waited for us to
understand. We would all go to a bowling alley after
the Thursday exercise, we'd slap him on the shoulder,
tell him stupid dirty jokes; it never occurred to us to
invite him for dinner, in the restaurant he paid his own
way.

Catherine says that when the first camping trip
was organized to Morocco in the summer of 64, everybody remained at the cafe terraces between Paris and
Tangier, waiting for Agha to give instructions. Since
he never said a word, everybody sat there looking at
each other for two weeks before starting on the trip
back home.

Even though our attitude towards Agha often
veered between infantile dependence and brash over-
familiarity, he took it all with kindness, hiding any
impatience he may have felt. To be fair, not everyone
was like this. The above mentioned Bella had understood what the scale of a Master was, but since she was
the "crazy woman" of the group, we weren't going to
be convinced. Her childhood playground was the
camp at Auschwitz and she died young of bone cancer.

1965 was the year of the trip to Turkey and

Konya: both Shah and Agha were there. I myself was now working as a salesman in the shop, when not dubbing films and acting in the theater.

The first Paris Tekkia was installed above the shop in the Passage Saint-Andre (it's a tea-room today). After the inauguration, Agha moved back to England with his young wife. On the group trip to Granada in 67, at the campsite outside of town, an English enthusiast was searching everywhere for a Sufi teacher and his disciples who he had been told were at a camping ground in Granada: the proprietor replied that there was nobody of that description here, just families with children. Agha walked his baby and put up a tent to shade the little girl during her siesta: it didn't occur to us that we should help him, in fact I remember him shinnying up a tree to attach a tent cord for me and repairing my ancient car: it seemed normal that he should wait on me. The Englishman never found us until the day before we were leaving to go back.

It would be impossible to exaggerate the euphoria we were in at this time. We had the run of the candy store: a two-headed Master in the form of Agha and Shah, both of them extraordinary, the English and French group were one, two shy Spaniards had attached themselves to us, South America or the United States had not yet joined the caravan, and we thought quite sincerely that the work had already been done and that all we had to do to gather its fruits was to hold out our arms.

In 1967 the Rubayyat of Omar Khayyam was published by Cassell's in a new translation by Robert Graves and Omar Ali Shah. Robert Graves was then the most famous English language poet alive, and Agha being associated with him gave him probably the highest press and public profile he will ever have. In fact, the translation was almost entirely Agha's: Grave's contribution to the text represented probably no more than a dozen minor suggestions. Grave's implicitly recognized this when he declared during the furor that followed this "desecration" of a hallowed text, that the proposal to be co-author of the translation was "the highest poetic compliment I have ever been paid".

Now that the Sufi influence is completely recognized throughout Arab and Persian classical literature and civilization, it is difficult to imagine the bomb-like effect of this translation and the anger it provoked. Fitzgerald's version, although completely contradicting the original Omar Khayyam text, was regarded as sacrosanct: generations of British children had been brought up on it, what did it matter if Fitzgerald had turned it into an anti-religious tract: why was one to care about these two weirdos who were claiming that the concept of "wine" was a symbol of the drunken state one enters into when one begins to know God? So what if Fitzgerald was anti-religious, what was all the fuss about?

The polemic which then began was carefully nurtured with letters for and against from friends, and replies to the replies to the replies in the letter columns. The names of Agha and Shah were dragged in the mud: who the hell were these Afghans from nowhere, who had no Institution or University teaching job behind them?

Worst of all, Shah's books were becoming best-sellers at the time, and Tom Maschler at Jonathan Cape wanted to turn him into the successor of the Maharishi. The English orientalist running the institutions and the educational system, who had the market cornered, could only sell their books by the hundreds: they took a very dim view of this upstart taking over their turf. Endless bickering took place about the authenticity of the manuscript used for the translation, and Agha was challenged to produced the original Persian text: in the event, he decided that he would refuse to play along with people such as these, and he never did produce the manuscript.

At the Easter meeting in 1968 Agha produced the first of a number of shock-waves when he asked us to stand up and be counted if we were engaged in the Sufi work, which would henceforth no longer be known as the "Work" as with the Gurdjieffians, but as the "Tradition".

He had never asked us for any over demonstration of this kind: we were all dignified and well-behaved people; some of us were even intellectuals. He then told us that he was going to have to stop taking care of us. I never believed him for a moment: such an idea was inconceivable. Maybe he was talking to only some of us: this incident has always remained an enigma to me. I can't explain it and I had better not try.

Perhaps the incidents of this period represent a sort of litmus test, i.e. an evaluation by the two brothers about how the Sufi Tradition was going to "take" in the West. In any case, from that time on, the two brothers followed different roads, or "agreed to disagree" as Agha put it to us.

Agha himself has written "As far as agreeing to disagree with I. Shah, it was a simple matter but a fundamental one: he is the theorist concerned with projecting the Tradition in a way that it would be "acceptable" to Academics and other professional philosophers and intellectuals".

In this letter Agha goes on to say: "I am not a theorist. I know what I am trained to teach and communicate and carry out, and I do it in the most efficient way, I do not seek "approval" from Western thinkers. I do not want honorary degrees and academic applause. My first responsibility is to those people who put their trust in me, and if I have to use a particular, even shocking or strange activity, in order to communicate knowledge or energy, i will do it even if it may cause people to be scandalized". (Letter of 4.10.86)

The first junction that took place between our new friends from South America and ourselves was during the group trip to Assisi in the summer of 69. We thought they were very nice but we found them a little over-enthusiastic in the way they expressed themselves. Bernard L. went so far as to encourage them to "liberate" certain artifacts in a nearby church: he was politely thanked and sent off on his own in September.

The births of our two sons meant that Catherine and I did not attend trips between 1970 and 73. Throughout this time Agha pushed hard to start off groups in South America: work in Mexico had begun, groups were organized on behalf of Agha in Italy, and there was a strong expansion into Germany. The new groups in Mexico, Brazil and Argentina had great vitality and enthusiasm and their people were completely different in temperament to the Anglo-French elements that had made up the ex-Gurdjieff group in Paris, and the perception they had of the way one worked was also completely different.

In 71/72 the axe fell: "My brother and I have agreed to disagree on the projection of the teaching in the West". What appeared unthinkable at the time seems fairly logical with hindsight. What was confusing at the time, and which still confuses people even today, is the fact, as Irina Hoare puts it, that "many people, once bitten by the Tradition, cannot ever leave it, even though they are not able to find enough trust to

xiv

commit themselves completely to a Master". There are always a lot of people waiting in the wings convinced they have a starring role: it is also such people who tend to find their way into print, and who become "experts" on the subject for the outside world.

When the two channels decided to separate, many people were left in the middle, because they had no real conviction at all. Many of the people who had been rather happy with the rather austere power based work of the Gurdjieffians could not bear calling into question what they had done for so long.

When Agha began to introduce prayer-like invocation in Arabic before the exercise, this really "separated the men from the boys": there are in fact very few people still with us from the large anglophone contingent of this time.

Agha pushed very hard in Spain and in Latin America, many new members came into the Tradition and work began on the building of new Tekkias (or dervish meeting houses).

From the perspective of twenty years, it can be seen that Agha's way of working has indeed been in a more classical mould than his brother's: group meetings, prayers in the Arab language, collective exercises and activities, and the encouragement of a feeling of belonging and identification which is almost military in nature. While not participating directly in Idries Shah's teaching operation, my feeling is that it took place directly between the person and his or her mentor, with books as a primary contact, and that using a group as a tool or relay mechanism was less important for whatever technique he used.

At Easter 76, the Brazilian and Mexican friends joined us at Pierrefitte. The weather was horribly cold and it was snowing. The friends, who were without overcoats, fresh from the South American summer were put up on the floor of the Church Hall without any heating, and the members of the Paris group retired to their heated hotel rooms for the night.

Across the street from the Church, the large warm house of one of our friends remained empty so that Agha and Anna, who were staying there, would be able to have a place to get away to. Perhaps our foreign friends were able to see the delicate supper being prepared as they swigged down the Tequila they had bought as the only possible remedy against the invading cold. The next morning members of the Paris group smelt the alcohol on their breaths, and found this quite shocking: these South Americans really didn't know how to behave. When word later got back to us about how our friends didn't feel us to be very hospitable, our reaction was that such people lacked respect towards their elders in the Tradition.

At the Arcos Easter meeting of 78 an incident took place which gave me much food for thought: on the last evening, among the many Brazilian and Spanish friends who were seeing Agha for the first time, a show of songs and dances was organized which ended in a near-riot with everyone screaming "Agha! Agha!".

With his usual calm, he then came up on stage and proceeded to praise the selflessness of his wife in words that could have been taken from the mouth of any professional politician on the campaign trail. There was of course an immediate feedback: the whole room rocked to the cries of "Anna! Anna!" and people began to jump up on the tables and stamp their feet. The tables were on movable struts and they began to fall over, and one of the Brazilian friends was caught underneath while above her the others went on stamping: she ended up with a broken leg. I glanced over at the object of all this adoration: Anna's face was a study in white terror, she was poleaxed. The anglo friends began to look first at each other, then at the surrounding craziness: was this really what they wanted? A few months lather, they had all bowed out.

And why did I not follow them out, even though I was by no means a fan of this kind of thing? Simply because, when I talked to the friends who had "led" this episode the next day, I realized that this "spontaneous" event had been organized, it had not happened just by accident, it had been carefully planned and orchestrated. My curiosity was too strong to let go at that point: I wanted to know why.

Fourteen years later, I think I'm beginning to come up with at least the beginning of an answer which satisfies me although I quite understand that it may not be satisfactory to others. This is it: once one starts of a process of overly grandiose self-identification, a concomitant process of this grandiosity's self-destruction is set off at the same time: I would consider this a more or less inescapable law. If, as an individual, one has associated oneself too closely with this grandiosity, one will feel that one's essential being is being destroyed along with this useless shell. One then either swallows hard and gets on with it, or else one walks away in a tiff. Some stay, others walk away.

The application of this law takes place at every level and should not be considered a purely intellectual concept. It applies to every area of one's own behavior, as well as to the relationship with one's teacher. In any real Tradition, one is ultimately forced to define the limits of one's own commitment to the teacher and to the Tradition, and non-conventional or shocking behavior by the teacher is an indispensable part of the array of techniques available, so that the teacher can ensure that this testing process takes place:

if a teacher did not test a pupil's trust, he or she would be cheating the pupil by preempting the pupil's ever-present option to leave.

When viewed from outside, as in the above incidents I have related, the normal cynical and/or conditioned view will be that the teacher in engaged in a process of self-interested manipulation: it is only when one has been able to experience the workings of the Sufi Tradition over a long period of time that one begins to realize how the time factor meshes into the individual situations and perceptions, and effects its change on the basic human material involved.

One of the hardest things for a Westerner to do is to learn to trust his or her teacher, because the entire western intellectual tradition (with a small "t") is based on developing a sceptical and narrowly analytical view of reality. In the Sufi Tradition we would consider such a thing to be part of the inevitable environmental or social conditioning one is subjected to, and which must be overcome.

It is therefore hardly surprising that academics, whose strength is rarely humility, react by saying "Who do these Sufis think they are, looking down at us!". In fact, we are only saying that we are not the proprietors of knowledge, only its servants, and that Western education has got its priorities wrong, because information only begins to have some value once a basis of self-knowledge has been achieved.

This begs the question: what is self-knowledge? Now everybody has his own answer to such a question insofar as it applies to themselves, and everyone is probably right: suffice it so to say that such a knowledge is regarded in the Sufi Tradition as being worthy of a lifetime's study and work. Belief enters into this picture, because there has to be some kind of measuring rod that enables us to at least aspire to perfection, whether or not our destiny is to attain it.

If one looks at it in this way, one can consider that a Sufi teacher and a Sufi group are simply technical instruments designed to provide a relay between an individual and a higher order of knowledge. In order to become engaged in such a process, one must assume for the time being that, at least theoretically, such a higher knowledge, which can be connected to a knowledge of the personal self, does exist.

Let us be very clear about the limits to any philosophy or way of thought: the Sufi Tradition, as such, cannot create self-knowledge, cannot create belief, cannot create trust, and did not and cannot create an awareness of God. Nevertheless, it is a technique which can be used by any individual person, whatever his or her background or capacity, to build upon and add to any of the above. But as Omar Ali-Shah points out time and time again, "I cannot do the work for you".

Some people, when reading about people breaking their legs or sleeping on the floor in the cold, may say "What does this have to do with spiritual development? These people are savages!". The only answer I can give to such a reaction is: "Yes, but I aspire to something else. I may be a savage at the present time, but with the help of God and the Tradition, I will not always be this way".

The duty of a Sufi teacher is to do what has to be done: he does not necessarily have the time or the inclination to explain himself. In any case, things can only be explained up to a point.

Augy Hayter

Chapter 1

The Characteristics of the Tradition

The nature of the Sufi Tradition is one of brothers and sisters united in an effort. It is a free association of people who enter into the Tradition freely and who can also leave freely. If they separate themselves from the Tradition, we do not consider them to be excommunicated, rejected, damned, and all sorts of nonsense like that. They are free to come and free to go. If they go, we are sorry that they have gone. If they are separated, we maintain the contact. Yet when they are actively concerned with the activities of the Tradition, then they must follow in a dedicated and disciplined fashion.

In the Tradition, they are responsible to me, responsible to the person or persons to whom I have given the authority to supervise activities, and responsible to themselves. I can be present with them all the time, one of my deputies can be present and available to them, but their greatest responsibility is toward themselves. If they do not feel that responsibility, if a person does not find out how they can be responsible to themselves, then they can leave before the pressure becomes too great.

That is not to say that the pressure becomes so enormous that there's a danger of them going mad or something like that. The Tradition does not operate in the areas of madness, with threats and menace. We tell people what is possible, and we teach them how to achieve the possible. I will push or pull people, I will talk to people, cry for people, and do whatever is necessary in order to help them, I will laugh at them and with them, but I will not do their work for them.

In the Tradition we call it a path or a voyage. If I have been on that voyage, along that path, I can tell people the way, I can tell them the problems they are likely to find, and what activities or terms of reference they can use when they are faced by them. I do not make the voyage for them, neither should anybody expect me to do so.

I will tell you : I am a professional, I'm not an amateur; I am not, thank God, an intellectual. I'm a professional and a pragmatist. If I say anything, it is usually based on my personal knowledge and experience. I don't deal in vague, supernatural theories : they can be very exciting and they give you an adrenaline boost, but it's like a firework, it exhausts itself quickly. If you want a permanent "high" and excitement, look elsewhere.

If people think "He is painting a black picture of suffering, doom and horror" : no, I'm dealing in practical activities, in positive and useful potential. I'm not going to paint pretty pictures of marvellous rosy and heavenly vistas. I'm not a stick-or-carrot man, reward or punishment, "do it or else." If I say "do it or else" I will tell you plainly and clearly what the alternative is. I have learned in a very hard school, and I continue to learn. As we say in my country "My hair did not become white by sitting in the sun." I know better than to leave anything to people's so-called intellect or imagination. I don't gamble with people's happiness or sanity, or my own.

When I insist on certain values and terms of reference being used, it is because in my experience these are tried, useful and correct techniques, and in the Tradition we are following a technically exact and disciplined activity. Everything we do, everything we use, our music, our zikrs, our colour combinations, are technical instruments within the overall context of the Tradition.

Yes, some of these instruments are surrounded by a mass of esoteric "weeds", for lack of a better word. If you're using a correct and delicate technical instrument, there is no place for esoteric nonsense. Then comes the question "How then do you define esoteric or esotericism? How do you define natural or supernatural?" I don't define it. I undefine what is called esotericism. You see, unfortunately, terms like "esoteric" or "supernatural" have gone into the realm of mystic floating-around and "third eye", and have become completely inexact. You say "esoteric" and everybody says

The Characteristics of the Tradition

"Ah yes" and they're thinking of everything from Noah's Ark to goodness knows what. After a good dinner and a few beers, you say to somebody "I am going to tell you something esoteric". Everybody looks very conspiratorial and their eyes glaze over, because they're "into esotericism" : end of lesson and useful conversation.

We who teach and you who learn have inherited a perfectly technical path. Every teaching in the books of the great Masters of the Tradition is a technique : all are technical textbooks. Yes, to understand them and to practise what they're teaching you have to develop terms of reference. We owe the great Masters a very great debt of gratitude; they have left us an enormous store of useful wisdom. We should use that wisdom and that technique. There is a saying that a wise man who does not use his wisdom is like a donkey with a load of books.

These are tried and proved techniques. With some, one can understand them fully and use them immediately. With some, every time one uses them, they become more and more familiar, whereas others keep themselves hidden until the person is capable of understanding how they function. There is obviously a good technical reason for this. If it were not a question of time and effort, you could be giving people powers and energies that they are not capable of using correctly. This would be irresponsible : it would be the equivalent of giving a child of five a loaded machine-pistol.

Your capacity to use techniques becomes greater, as well. Using the Tradition's terms of reference or activities in the context of the Tradition becomes automatic. I don't like to use this word because "automatic" implies a sort of robot, puppet reaction and this is completely contrary to what we are trying to achieve. When I say one must learn to use techniques in the context of the Tradition I mean exactly that. In the Tradition we are taught to be in the world and not of the world.

If you say "I have a hundred dollars, shall I buy a tasbee or shall I pay my electricity bill?" you really shouldn't be asking that sort of question. Don't take my word for it, try it. Buy one, you're sitting at home happily using your

Sufism for Today

tasbee, and a man comes and knocks at your door and says "I want a hundred dollars for your electricity" and you say "Go away, I am a Sufi and I have a tasbee, and he says "How very interesting" and cuts off your electricity. So you sit there in the dark with your rosary and you blame the insensitive fool : this is a lack of precision in thinking and action.

You could say "I have a hundred dollars, I will buy a small tasbee for fifty and I will pay half my electricity bill, or I can buy an even smaller tasbee and pay seventy-five dollars for my electricity bill; or I can use a hundred dollars to pay the electricity bill and have the electricity to work and keep warm and earn enough money to buy a tasbee." I don't personally think that a choice like that should be a source of great confusion, and yet people fall into these situations all the time. "I have ten thousand dollars", I promise you these are questions that are asked to me : "from the point of view of the Tradition is it better that I open a pizza parlour or sell kilims?"

Don't ask me, ask your bank manager, and he'll probably say "You owe me five thousand dollars, pay that and invest the other five thousand in supporting yourself or your family." When dealing with that area, check out the commercial possibilities of the situation, don't mix energies. In the context of the Tradition we use very precise, carefully processed and distilled energy, not crude energy. Just as the muscles of the human body function with a certain portion of galvanic current, the brain and the nervous system also use galvanic currents which are very tiny, very precisely measured quantities in comparison to that which is used by the larger muscles. The more sophisticated the brain area, the more pure the energy has to be : you cannot mix the two currents. They can and do run parallel in the human body; they help and complement each other. If you plug the galvanic energy from these muscles straight into your brain, say because you want to think more deeply and quickly or whatever, you won't blow your brain apart, but a fuse will go. And the result of having tried to do that will be confusion, depression, and general vagueness.

4

The Characteristics of the Tradition

Now all of these things are familiar, so I don't have to describe what they feel like. "All is well, I can do anything I like and Agha will look after me" : yes, I have given my word, and I will do so, but I am not in the business of constantly repairing people's fuses. I'll repair them once or twice; I will explain directly or indirectly how and why they blew, but I will not stand around with a hammer and nails every time somebody has some ludicrous and idiotic idea which blows his or her fuse. I have said it before and I will say it again : I am there for everybody, wherever they may be, whatever the question of distance, location, or time; but not with a hammer and nail. I am as far away and as near as a person wishes me to be. I have used, I can use, and I will use every possible technique available to me. I cannot think of any situation where I cannot find a correct technique.

So I am an arrogant megalomaniac. As to whether I'm a megalomaniac or not, there are many ways of discovering whether I in fact am this or not : one way is to compare anything I say or do with any of the writings of the past great masters. If I say or do anything which is contrary to what they have said or done, then I am in error.

Another extremely important aspect of the Tradition is communication between me and the individuals in various groups, as well as communication within the group. The responsibility of the senior members of a group towards the younger or newer members is very considerable. In terms of time and length of contact, the older friends are a fundamental link between the newer members of the group and the Tradition itself. Whether they have recently come in or have been involved for some time, everybody has questions or sometimes confusions about various things. It is the distinct responsibility of the Naibs, the Murshids, the Murshidas, to identify constantly these questions or areas of confusion.

That doesn't mean looking through people's windows, tapping people's telephones, examining their mail, or telephoning them day and night; it means establishing, maintaining and developing deep contact : seeing incorrect terms of reference or incorrect behaviour before it comes up or as it develops, and taking the necessary steps to correct

5

the situation. It is not efficient to be ignorant of the fact that somebody is thirsty, to be unaware of the development of his or her thirst, and then finally and very hurriedly get a bucket of water and throw it over the person. If you think carefully, precisely and efficiently, you can act in a similar way. If you allow yourself time and are patient with yourself, you then have time to examine your own possibilities, compare them with the situation, and do something positive. Positive action using positive energy must produce a positive result. A negative action with a negative intention must produce a negative result.

You should not and you cannot efficiently take bits and pieces of the Tradition which you like, or which are nice. You take it all, you practise it all, or you practise none of it. There is an English story which is called the Curate's Egg. According to the story, the Vicar was having breakfast with the Curate, and the Vicar was very mean and bought things very cheaply if he could, and the food really wasn't very good. So it happened on that day that they had boiled eggs for breakfast, and the Curate was picking at his egg a little bit carefully, and the Vicar said to him : "Is there anything wrong with your egg?" And the Curate said: "No, no, parts of it are excellent."

The totality of the Tradition is excellent. It is demanding. It demands loyalty to the Tradition and loyalty to each other within the context of the Tradition. I will personally, in any situation, back you individually and collectively all the way, but equally, if you are dishonest to yourself or yourselves, I will drop you just as quickly. We are living and acting in an adult world. We use technical and adult terms of reference.

Communicate, produce the energy, share the energy, receive the energy. The energy is there, the path is there, the technique is there : put these together with correct intention and you can achieve things which are beyond your wildest imagination.

A young man went to a Sufi teacher who worked as a blacksmith, and he said to the Sheikh : "I've been told that you can produce gold from base metal." So the Sheikh said

"Yes, why do you ask?" And the young man said "Can you teach me, maybe?" And the Sheikh said "Yes, stay around a little bit and I'll teach you" and the years passed. And a few more years passed, and occasionally the young man said "Er, ahem, you know, this gold thing, how you make it?" and the Sheikh said: "We'll get round to that, carry on doing what you're doing and I'll work it out" and more years passed. One day they were working side by side on the workbench, and the Sheikh said to him "By the way, I'm going to teach you to make gold today" : the young man, intent on what he was doing, said "Yes, yes, thank you very much, I don't need it really, some other time".

So, that actually is to stop anybody saying to me : "Agha, I have a bit of a problem with my bank, could you tell me how one makes gold?" You'll get exactly the same answer from me as the young man got. That is not to say that you have to then become terribly clever and come up and say: "You know all about this gold-making business, I'm not worried about that, tell me what comes after" because there is lesson one, and then lesson two, and then lesson three. Nasrudin wanted to learn to play the flute, so he asked a flute teacher "Can you teach me to play as well as you? And the flute teacher said to him " I can do it, but you have to pay for the lessons." So Nasrudin said to him "Fine, how much do you charge for each lesson?" And the man said to him that the first lesson was one gold piece and the second lesson was one silver piece, and Nasrudin said "Fine, here is a silver piece, I'll have the second lesson."

Don't be afraid to ask if you don't know. If you do ask, think first, and work out a correct question. I don't want to hear a question from anybody prefaced with the story of their lives and everything else they can think of leading up to it : "Oh I can't ask that question, Oh it's so stupid, Oh I'm embarrassed." I have had questions put to me which would make your teeth fall out.

The fact that you ask a question of me, or of a Naib or Murshid does not necessarily mean that you will get an answer. It certainly does not mean that you will get the answer which you either want or expect. You can, and people do, spend a lot of time cleverly manufacturing an incredibly complex question, and wait in ambush, and spring it on me at a moment that they think is propitious. They will very probably receive a look from me of abysmal lunacy with the jaw dropping, that is, if they are lucky. If I'm not my normal gentle self, the reaction might be somewhat different.

I insist on the precise formulation of a question for two very good reasons : firstly, the precision of a question reflects a precise thought pattern. Secondly, and very usefully indeed, in formulating the question the person will in fact very often find the answer for themselves.

If anybody asks how a profound aspect of the Tradition could be expressed in a short and simple phrase, I will give you one. There is a short formula which expresses the very fundamental aspect of the Tradition : harmonious balance, harmonious equilibrium. A correct balance does not necessarily mean no movement at all, there is inevitably a seesaw, up-and-down motion. But it should not be a great degree of up-and-down ; if anything, it should be a tremor rather than an earthquake.

One of the fundamental laws of the Galaxy has to be equilibrium. Can you imagine the result of a democratic choice of planetary orbits? It would not be a pretty sight, assuming anybody survived to witness it. If we are part of the Galaxy, why should we be arrogant enough to consider that we should not obey these fundamental laws? It is a baseless arrogance to think that one should not obey such things. If you're conscious of arrogance and it is firmly based on something, it is possible to use it. If this arrogance is not based on a solid foundation, it will most certainly and inexorably let you down when you rely on it most. If your arrogance is subordinate to your technique, it can be useful. If your baseless arrogance controls you, then the result will inevitably be negative.

Why do I keep talking about arrogance? Because it takes many forms. Arrogance is not a developed pride. If a person does something efficiently and well, when it is finished he has every reason for what we call quiet pride. Baseless

The Characteristics of the Tradition

arrogance can be shown by an unjustified pride in one's own capacity. Arrogance can show in the way one dresses, in the way one talks and in one's attitude. People can and do fall over their own false pride and arrogance, and they can be surprised, shocked or confused if they do so.

Maybe it is because they look upon it as some alien creation which has come from somewhere to confuse them. If they can identify it truly for what it is, then they can hunt it down. Look at a situation or at yourself from a correct perspective. Examine yourself patiently with correct terms of reference, and you will get a positive result every time. Behave or examine yourself with impatience and with incorrect terms of reference and you'll have a problem.

Don't let yourself down. Don't be dishonest to yourself. If you are, you will come up against me : I don't recommend it.

■

Chapter 2

The Concept of Master
in the East and West

One of the significant problems which faces us in transmitting the Tradition in the West is one which is due to a lack of positive conditioning, rather than to the presence of the negative conditioning I normally complain about.

The word and concept of "Master" or "Teacher" is a familiar thing in almost any oriental country, whether it be a Muslim, Hindu, Buddhist, Shinto or any other society based on some basic belief. People grow up in the Orient with the word "teacher" or "Master" as familiar to them as "bus driver", "priest", "milkman" or any other functionary; and the existence of a teacher or Master is a very close and obvious thing to them, either because their family has connections with a particular philosophical doctrine and that they are familiar with the word teacher or Master, or because they have themselves been in touch in early life or at some other time with such a teacher. This means that when the word teacher or Master is mentioned, the whole concept is already clear. If you say to the average European child at the age of four or five : "The milkman is coming" or "You have to go and see the dentist, doctor" or something like that, the whole concept of what that means is immediately evoked, and they understand the function of that particular person : how he relates to them, how he influences them as a doctor, how he cures them, how as a dentist he takes out their teeth, how as a milkman he delivers the milk.

So these trigger words or occupations, if you like, raise no particular problem in the Orient because if one refers to somebody as the "Master so-and-so", it immediately conjures up the concept of what that person's function is, and there is no confusion.

In a recent conversation, I took an example going quite far back into the Middle Ages : the first western country in which you had the people who were called "God's fools" or "wise madmen" or people like that, was in Russia. You had these wandering preachers, priests, anchorites, and so forth who delved into the various aspects of esoteric and exoteric areas of the Christian religion. They were not really considered Masters, but rather as teachers and thinkers : some of them were considered as "holy fools" : but the existence of such people and their influence as teachers became familiar to the people of Russia earlier on than to the people further West.

This was due to the fact that the exposure to the teaching of the Tradition took a considerable time to penetrate into the West. It was a question of time-scale, of the ability to travel; routes were opened up, travelling became safer. Much of the intermingling of peoples and so forth, albeit interrupted by occasional Crusades and things like that, really started out from the Middle East, the Levant, what is now the Lebanon and Syria and went across North Africa, extending from North Africa up through Sicily, influencing Italy, the South of France, and eventually Moorish Spain.

During that time, there was a highly developed philosophical exchange of ideas between the various Christian orthodoxies in Europe and Islam; and the amount of exchange between scholars of the two sides of the known world was quite admirable. The language they had in common was Latin : Arabs learnt Latin and could correspond with Divines and other people in the West, and many learned Christian travellers and other people went to the Orient and learned Arabic.

If you look at a 10th or 11th century map of the world, you will find that there are areas of Europe, the Middle East and Central Asia which were in intimate contact with each other. The first contact was travelling, hence the interchange of ideas and the discussing of the various philosophies : trade and other things came later. Some of the earliest voyages of Russian monks to Central Asia and to Afghanistan, then into Kashmir, are very well documented, and many of them stayed for many years before returning, so that there was an exchange of information going on.

But with the proliferation in Russia of what some people called the ecstatics and others called the Illuminati : some people called them less polite names : there was an unfortunate element of abuse which can very easily creep into a thing like this. Sometimes an anchorite who had been sitting in a cave for fifteen years thinking great thoughts and being looked after by the locals would come out of his cave and set fire to the village, or maybe burn down everything he could get his hands on. Now in fact, someone like this was raving mad : nevertheless, on some occasions, this gave the anchoriteship, or whatever the term is, a bad reputation.

At a point when they were arriving at the stage of interchanging ideas, philosophies, esoterica; and getting to use the techniques of meditation, prayer and so forth, people were gradually introducing the idea that there existed a teaching Tradition which could and should and would be carried out in the West. Yet there were occasions when this pattern would be disturbed by some nutty anchorite, who, claiming some sort of vague philosophy, went out and butchered or ate somebody, or did something horrible, and he then put back this status one step.

At the same time you had the introduction of the word "Master" into the languages of Europe. In medieval Europe this word had acquired an unfortunate connotation : it meant master and servant, master and slave, master and serf, i.e. someone who belonged body and soul to the person who happened to own the place and who had no rights or anything like that at all.

It was necessary to differentiate between the political or feudal authority implied by the word "master" and the Master as a teacher. This was, and up to the present day, still is, very difficult; because of the master/servant conditioning and hence what the word master has come to imply.

In the Middle Ages, one had mad anchorites doing all sorts of terrible things; and since the eighteen-sixties, we have had people travelling around, coming out of Asia or out of holes in the wall, claiming to be some sort of master or other. Those who had no justification for doing so and who took advantage of and therefore abused that title did a disservice to the whole concept.

In the present-day West you have had any number of cults which have sprung up, and they all have some relationship with a meditative spiritual development, inner development, or self-harmonising technique. Unfortunately, a large number of them have simply been cults, and one has seen the disastrous results that some of them have caused. Every time something like this happens, the name "Master" has a bit of the varnish knocked off it : people say "Well, here comes another one."

You might say "Surely, this type of abuse must have happened in the Orient. You're not telling me that there are no loonies there or people who take advantage of others in the East?" There were and are such people, but it was more difficult or even impossible there, because in the Orient this was all taking place within a Buddhistic, Taoist, Hindu or Islamic concept : if a person put himself forward or declared himself a Master, the people around him knew about his line of authority.

They knew his ancestral line of descent, who he was a pupil of, who taught him, what he belonged to. It was all public knowledge, because all the people who were involved in an esoteric environment or who had esoteric connections would either know or could easily verify the claims of a person who turned up in a cloud of smoke or something like that, and said "I am the great Whodunnit. They would be able to say "Fine, what is your authority?" "Well, I'm the great Whodunnit and I'm the pupil of the great Whowasit, who was a pupil of Whodidn't-knowwhat" and they would politely say "Buzz off" or words to that effect.

Now in our own Tradition we talk about the Silsila, which basically means "the line of descent of authorized teachers" either of a particular school in the Tradition, or within the sort of overall command structure. The various schools or orders like the Naqshbandi, Mevlevi, Suhrawardi,

Qadiri and others usually take their names from the Master-teacher who established a form of training within the overall format of the Tradition. For instance, you can have different methods of exercise, or a diversity of techniques for creating an ambiance which will be used by different groups working within all of the Sufi orders, but their function is, in fact, the same.

You have the Chisti, who clap; the Rifai, who howl; the Mevlevi, who whirl; there are ones who whistle, and all sorts of things like that. The functional basis of all these different orders, their zikrs, their exercises, are for the same purpose : they take place within the same context. Whether they differ in the performance of particular exercises or zikrs, whether some of them recite aloud or silently, or whether some have distinguishing colours on their robes and others have not is not relevant to the efficacy otherwise of their activities, or else you would be justified in saying: "Right, I will go in for the noisy howlers, because that appears to be more expressive, rather than the wretched Naqshbandis who just sit there and say nothing." Well, what is seen to be done and what is actually done is a different thing.

Within the Tradition, the Silsila is the Master-pupil relationship which has directly come down to us, and it includes among it Masters who introduced techniques, updates, or modifications of techniques as and when they were needed; but always keeping to the main line of the Tradition as we know it.

In terms of the hierarchical situation, each different order is administratively independent. You have the Sheikh and you have the High Sheikh. When a person achieves the rank of High Sheikh of an order within the Sufi Tradition, he is automatically considered to be the High Sheikh of all the other orders, that is to say he has reached a stage where, from where he is, he has a full knowledge of what the overall aims and objectives are; this includes the particular confidential or secret activities of the other orders. It is part of his function to know such things so that he may better harmonize the activity of all the different orders.

So the High Sheikh of the Qadiris is certainly on the same level as the High Sheikh of the Mevlevis, in the sense that he shares the knowledge of how and where the Mevlevis operate, so that he can complement their activities within his Qadiri order. The High Sheikhs themselves are subordinate to the Auliyas or Abdals, of whom there are forty, and they in turn are subordinate to the four Pillars or Qutubs.

Within this system there is sometimes a lot of confusion. People come hotfooting along and say : "Oh, I've been to Baghdad or Damascus or somewhere and I got a zikr or a tape from somebody of the Khallawati Order or something like that : can I, should I, or how do I use it?"

Just as every order has certain different ways of organizing meetings or exercises, so different orders use different instruments. Broadly speaking, the orders share two main intruments : one is the tasbee and the other is the robe. Yes, there are the kashkuls which belong to different orders, there are sticks, stones, caps, belts and other things; but the two basic and essential intruments which are used by every order are the tasbee and the robe.

There is no such thing as a good, bad, or better tasbee. The material of which a tasbee is made makes a slight difference in the sense that some materials hold, generate, use and transmit energy better. Different orders will tend to have a different form of pompom on the end, but this is irrelevant.

If the intention is lowered, if one says "Oh I couldn't touch that, that is a Qadiri tasbee," one is getting into a social area, i.e. "It's from Woolworths, I want a Harrod's one." If the intention is there, one can use a pile of pebbles : the Prophet use pebbles. That's why the Wahabi Saudis officially outlaw the tasbee, because they say it's innovative. The Prophet had two piles of pebbles and he took one from one side to the other, so that the tasbee can be said to be innovative, therefore they consider it should be not used.

Back to the robe again; the different colours show the affiliation of the person to the particular order. It is also a matter of convenience : a person can be identified by that, and a contact can be made. Various colours are added in stripes to the robe; these colours are shared among all Sufi orders. Some use a particular color more than others, and it's considered Mevlevi blue or something like that, but it's not as categorical as all that. The colours which are added to the robes assist in the use of the robe and they harmonize with each other.

Another function of the robe is that when someone wears it, it creates a microclimate around that person. It helps to hold in energy which the person themselves will produce, and it protects them from certain extraneous impacts which may be not dangerous, but could be disturbing. The third function of a robe is well-known : if a person is wearing one in a mosque or a tekkia or sitting in a field anywhere, it is a sign of the fact that they are meditating or doing an exercise, and that they don't want to be disturbed.

Colours are added to the robe. There are very distinct ways in which they are added : on the basis of seniority ; on the basis of how well they harmonize with the person, or for various different functions, for instance, to re-establish a certain equilibrium which the person may lack in their meditative or exercise activity.

By looking and reading, one sees and one learns that the various robes, colours, or caps worn by the different orders are really not secret. One learns to be able to recognize them, and to judge perhaps the seniority of a person, or from what order they come, or for how long they have been in the Tradition. The adding of colours to a robe should not be likened to Brownie badges : one for fire-lighting, one for climbing trees, one for knitting socks and so forth. They act in harmony with each other, and they also are deliberately confusing on occasions.

It is not a sacred object. It is accorded respect by people who know what it stands for, because they understand that the person who wears it is trying to develop and harmonize himself or herself, and he or she will therefore be accorded a certain amount of respect. It is never flaunted or worn to show off, and it is played down rather than played up.

Traditionally, when a robe is given, a small tear is made in the robe. It is a symbolic tear, a reminder of the fact that if someone wearing the robe and is feeling rather pleased with himself and is looked upon with envy by those who don't have one, he or she will always be conscious of the fact that their robe is torn.

■

Chapter 3

Defining and Recognizing Harmony

I am sure everybody is familiar with the concept of harmony. In some areas it is an abstract idea, especially in what one unfortunately calls the esoteric context. Since I try to be practical, I find that this word harmony has sometimes been over-used in an imprecise manner, as an abstract cultural context in art or music. I myself am concerned with the practical aspects : what does harmony or being harmonious mean within the context of the Tradition? Just simply that a human being, a product of this planet, should attempt to be in harmony with the other things that exist in this solar system. Under normal circumstances, most things on this planet work and exist in harmony with each other, whether they be animal, vegetable or material. The various forms of stone, vegetable matter, trees, flowers, animals, birds and so forth, establish a certain harmony in relation to each other.

Over the centuries and generations, man has assiduously cultivated a disharmony, very often because he has been told that man is different from the animals, and since he has things-like reasoning power, rationality or choice, he is therefore much better or different from mere animals, stones or flowers. This is a great arrogance. Why should man arrogate to himself the feeling, thought or position of being better? "God's greatest work" : well, opinions differ. Perhaps if one could get a first-hand definition from God Himself as to whether this is true, then it would be definitive, but in the absence of that, why should man consider himself any different?

So in comparison to other beings on this planet, man is rational, has thought processes, is capable of being educated, uses tools, instruments, techniques, and this sets him apart from the other things on this planet. Yes, perhaps he is developed in comparison to giraffes. Giraffes can't type, play the violin, but man can. Yet can a man produce small giraffes? No. So if the terms of reference are "Who can produce giraffes?" giraffes are superior to man. One is obviously not going to measure everything from the same point of view, nevertheless one can measure it from certain classic points of view, one of them being harmony.

Harmony means being in a position of compatibility, benefit and usefulness to the other things which constitute this planet. Just as this planet itself, as part of the solar system, is compatible in its movement, gravitational influence, potential and in other terms as well; it is harmonious, otherwise it is destroyed.

In the solar system or any other system for that matter, a maverick planet which goes out of its orbit, which oscillates, is literally pushed out : it either burns up or it freezes. It is put out from what one might call the comity of planets because it has declared a sort of unilateral independence : "I want to follow my own trajectory, apogee, perigee and so on, without reference to anybody else!" Its irresponsibility can have and in the past has had catastrophic effects, therefore its potential for destruction and disturbance is recognized, and the destruction or disturbance is prevented by salvatory action being taken.

In the context of a planet, a civilization or a people, say the human race, establishes a compatibility with its civilization and atmosphere, and all exist and develop within it, taking advantage of the natural substances, environment, animals, crops and food. They enhance their civilization in terms of agriculture and culture in all its various forms. At the same time, having established a basis of a developing civilization, they then harmoniously develop themselves within this context.

They do not abandon this once they have begun. For instance, take a ploughman, a shepherd or a minstrel : once a strolling player has learned a few tunes, and once the ploughman has learned to plough a straight furrow or the shepherd to look after sheep, he doesn't then abandon that and go on to be a professor of sheep-herding, emeritus instructor of ploughmanship. It is this sort of pecking order which produces the top-heavy situation. Fortunately the majority of people keep their sheep-herding working in tandem with an interior development : what we call being "in the world and not of the world." They don't abandon the old techniques either, because they're still useful, albeit updated : you no longer have two oxen pulling a wooden plough, you have a technologically developed plough behind a tractor. So man is still harmoniously developing his agriculture, using updated techniques, again within the context of profiting from the natural existence of things and being in harmony with them.

Once man has established what one might call a whole gamut of basic civilization, from scratching the earth and sowing seed to the most refined areas of culture, it must inevitably become obvious to him that he wants to become more closely in harmony with the things around him. He may define it differently : he may say that he is searching for his own identity for his relationship with humanity in general, or for his relationship with God : the way he defines it is not particularly important. What he should do is perceive it; perceive that it is necessary to develop harmoniously within the context of the planet, within the context of the solar system in which he finds himself, and to develop himself without detriment to his family, to other people, or to the society in which he lives.

In the Tradition, that implies that he does not go and live in a cave on a mountaintop. In one of these glorious phrases which come up, he may be "at peace with his soul" or something of that sort. Well, sitting in a cave on top of a mountain is probably very peaceful, but it is basically unproductive because a person is disengaged from his natural relationships. The temptation to do such a thing may be great, but from our point of view it is not particularly harmonious. He may consider that he can develop a certain harmony or tranquility within himself, but is it a tranquility of harmony or is it a tranquility of silence? The two things are compatible, but they shouldn't be absent from each other.

In this search for harmony, at some point a person should start to define, even somewhat hazily to begin with, some form of development that they consider could be available, and not to judge, to say "Well, I've read about this or that and I think I am capable of reaching such-and-such a point." This is a false start, because it depends on the teaching and on the amount of positive effort that a person puts in. They cannot say which point they are capable of reaching from the word go, because they will be imposing a limitation on themselves or boosting their hopes too high.

"I think I can reach the stage of Ignatius de Loyola" or whoever : if this is the pinnacle of one's hopes, it may be marvellous, yet one may be capable of even more. If they aspire to that, and in their estimation fall gravely short; it's a terrible disappointment; or if they suddenly find themselves looking down on the position occupied by Ignatius de Loyola, this could be a horrific experience to them. They could get scared and blow their minds.

One doesn't begin by saying : "Look, there is one particular part of my being which I want to specifically develop" because there is always the danger that this choice or priority may be influenced by any one of a number of aspects of conditioning which one has.

One might consider that one aspect is more important than another. Which is at the top of your hit list in terms of weaknesses?

Some particular weakness may be significant in that it comes out under varying circumstances, more or less constantly, according to a pattern. One might say : "Right, I have every reason to consider that this is the most important weakness, fallibility, or problem I have." One may be right, but it is a question of detached judgement. This is one of the earlier techniques of most activities in the Tradition, that is, to develop the capacity to detach oneself from oneself, and look at oneself under different circumstances and see how one reacted, and at that point, try and work out why.

Defining and Recognizing Harmony

If one looks at oneself in a reasonably detached and calm way, one can say in all honesty : "Right, some of the faults of character, action or attitude I have are as follows : laziness, impatience, inattention or whatever, and then one writes down a list of one's strengths and weaknesses : one becomes aware of the weaknesses and can therefore try to develop the strengths. This is, in fact, what one does in the context of the Tradition.

You're not looking for victims or to apportion blame, nor are you looking in order to satisfy yourself that "Yes, I was right, I am lazy or impatient or stupid" etc. If it was significant enough to come to the surface under various circumstances; when one has targeted it as being a significant area of weakness, or strength for that matter, it goes automatically onto one's priority list within oneself, and it is tackled.

There are exercises, readings, and activities to establish harmony with certain specific things : like places, with people, currents of energy, and with oneself at certain times and under certain circumstances. In working to achieve this harmony, one should not over-stress one specific harmony : that is to say one doesn't neglect the different areas where one is establishing a harmonic to the detriment of another, because then you get an im-balance.

We come back to this example I gave before, which is the hermit sitting in a cave on the mountain. A person may develop a very considerable harmony with them-selves after months or years in a cave, but after this period, should they then try to take their place among their family, friends or society, they will be out of harmony on basic things. Say the money ha been decimalized while they've been seven years in the mountains, so they come down and say "Can I have one-and-sixpence worth of toffee apples" and they are told "What? Do you mean eighteen p.?" It's a minor thing, but it goes though the whole area of disharmony : they have developed an imbalance. You can't call it an imbalanced harmony, be-cause by definition harmony is balance, it has to be.

Discord is not balance. If he comes down clothed in white, mystic and wonderful, and then goes into the village square and proclaims the Gospel, he will be thrown into the nuthouse straightaway or he will be shunned. This will cause alarm and despondency in himself and among other people, so that he is causing discord in various areas, not harmony.

So a person says "Okay, I think that I am capable of establishing harmony gently, that is in various areas within myself, within my society, in a global concept." A person should then try to do it in as many of the areas that are within his reach. He can be influenced by a way of thinking and a way of behaving which is learned, which is taken up, and which reflects on his thoughts, actions and plans.

Having made the firm decision that he is trying to follow a developmental path, a person does not immediately become commercially astute, physically perfect, economically a hundred percent stable, loved overnight by friends and enemies, and stars of stage and screen. Everything has to develop in a balanced and equilibrated way.

Aspirations : "I aspire to this, that or the other thing": these can be goals or aims; they are subject to modification, and can be flexible as one starts to be more conscious of one's strengths and weaknesses, as well as one's ability to use the energy which can become available.

In making a detached judgement when looking at oneself there is the question of individual conditioning : not everybody, by nature or background, is conditioned to the same extent by the same impacts. You can take six different people of different backgrounds, different ages, different education and so forth, put them in jail for six months, and they will all come out having been impacted upon differently. Some will use the six months to learn a trade, others will spend six months learning how to make counterfeit bank notes, some will have spent three months screaming and on a hunger strike, so there is no such thing as a specific layer of conditioning per year or anything of this sort.

Conditioning can be imposed by oneself or by circumstances during the course of a year, or even six months, and in the following six months, that layer can be removed by contact with something positive and useful : for instance by some positive activity. In criminology it is called rehabilitation : a fellow spends seven months in jail, then he comes out and is rehabilitated; he has paid his debt to society and he must be put on his feet. So the first year he spends out of jail, by dint of effort and social counselling and what have you, he is supposed to overcome the deprivation and other things which he has suffered during the months he was in prison.

People can be conditioned for a particular thing for ten years, and the amount of conditioning can theoretically be very thick, but that is not to say that this amount of conditioning cannot be removed within the succeeding ten months : because time is the funniest and very strange thing; it can be expanded or compressed: it is a qualitative entity, not a quantitative one, and providing one is acting within a correct and positive harmonious activity, it is redressing the imbalance. The amount of energy which one receives or produces will automatically be directed towards stimulating useful strengths and diminishing weaknesses which are detrimental to one's harmonious development. This is a big order and a big step: an uphill task in the sense that one has many years of conditioning, either self-imposed or imposed from outside, to overcome.

Harmony is the efficient and technical use of energy and the efficient and technical use of oneself in precise ways and areas in order to establish a harmony with oneself within the context that one lives, and with the aspiration to harmonize with those entities with whom one wishes to harmonize. Again, at the beginning stages, one doesn't necessarily have to make a list : "I want to harmonize with this that and the other thing" One can do it , it's not a terrible thing and it's not offensive to the effort, but only as long as they are penciled-in priorities and not fixed ones.

One prefers one piece of music to another, or one particular writer, colour, or material to another, fine. Possibly it's because one has established a harmony, possibly because this particular thing has impacted upon one at a given moment when one was at a stage of heightened awareness, and it has therefore taken hold in a valid sense. One has recognized the relationship with that person, object, music, colour, or whatever has been analyzed deeply : it has been found to be valid, and therefore it has become a part of one. It hasn't become an alien implant, because by definition, an alien implant is a de-harmonizing element.

Harmony is balance. Extremes are discord, as there is discord in music, as there is what can be considered discord in two inappropriate clashing colours or materials which by themselves may be valid within their own context. You don't force them together, you don't force harmony or accord.

So harmony is balance with nature, within the context of nature. I'm not talking about garlanding oneself with flowers and tripping through the woods, this is the extreme area of overly generalized harmonizing. It should not be abstract. "Oh, harmony's a wonderful thing" : yes, but feel it; just as when using the tactile sense one feels the harmony of a material, music, movement, activity or reading.

Try and bring the concept of harmony down from the theoretical area in order to use it and feel it. Feel a relationship, feel a harmonious situation, and try to influence them. Harmony is by no means a wishy-washy do-gooding type of thing, it is very tangible. It is as tangible as any considerable disharmony, say a knife skating across a plate. The other extreme is the "All things bright and beautiful", which is fine, I'm not selling it short; I rather like the hymn myself, but if one lived by it one would get trampled into the ground, either by oneself or by somebody else.

There is strength in harmony, yet you don't go into a place, or into yourself, and take out a club and say : " I'm going to harmonize you lot if I have to kill you" because this is then disharmony. If people are so inharmonious in general or to you in particular, either ignore them or kill them. Preferably ignore them, because killing is embarrassing and causes legal disharmony with all the situations it produces.

So you do not impose harmony in the form of an either/ or. You become harmonious by using harmonious techniques and knowing when you apply different types of harmony, insofar as suppleness and strength can both be harmonious in different circumstances. Hard and fast definitions generally lead to extremes.

Harmony is balancedunderstanding; a harmonious relationship with things around you. You do not have to go out and make a sort of great Crusade : "I hate my neighbor, but I'm going to harmonize with him." You can very easily harmonize with him in the nicest possible way by ignoring him. Harmony transmits and creates more harmony. Troubled minds, tensions and frustrations are inharmonious, but they all yield to harmony.

Yet harmony should not only mean the absence of disharmony. The absence of disagreement, quarreling, or falling-out does not necessarily mean harmony. What I am talking about is achieving common aims, common ideas, common attitudes, sharing them, and then using this harmony in a functional way. One has to build a positive situation in which the presence and use of harmony is a specific tool.

When one says in common terminology to "harmonize" with a situation, a person or with something, more often than not this means one sort of just gets on with a person. It should mean more than that, it should mean that one slots in with the person or, say, a piece of music: one harmonizes with it, and then on the basis of that harmony, you develop the situation, the harmony, the relationship, the context, further. It is not enough to say there is no disharmony. I reiterate this point because it is one which is very important, and often lost sight of : "Yes, yes, for goodness sake we are not quarreling, so what do we do now?" You don't non-quarrel, you do something with the non-quarreling situation.

By the use and injection of the energy you are establishing, you build on it further. If you have a fallow situation, maybe fallow in the sense of lack of weeds, lack of boulders; it will be a situation which should be capable of being developed, i.e. a situation and an attitude which is potentially beneficial. If it's potentially beneficial, why not develop its potential further rather than merely noticing that it exists : "It's perfectly all right, there are no weeds, there are no terrible stones, there is no problem, therefore it's okay." You should notice the fact that the particular relationship, situation, or ambiance is harmonious; it's good. You then look at it in relation to other situations, other people, other contexts and you see in what way you can increase the harmoniousness of the situation to harmonize with other things as well.

You do not develop some sort of paranoid necessity to harmonize everything, just as, take the analogy of a farmer who has several fields. One year he plants a root crop and wheat, and he leaves one field fallow so that he can rotate his crops from one to another. If he becomes paranoid about the fact that this field must yield crops, he'll spend his time rushing around putting in more and more crops, and sometimes he will produce more crops than he actually needs. This can increase his frustration because he's got this extra product he doesn't know what to do with, and it is an extra complication for him. But if he takes note that such-and-such a field this year will be fallow, it will rest the soil, be beneficial and, at that point, because it's in the scheme of things, this plot of useful land becomes part of the overall network of his activities; he's not worried about it, he knows that it's there.

If, during the course of a year, somebody comes along with a good idea of how he can use this land, he then looks at the whole picture and sees how it could possibly be used, how it could fit in with the rest of the scheme. At all times he is capitalizing on the availability of situations and functions. He's not running around saying he "must" do something with this land : nor is he just ignoring it, saying "Well, I can't think of anything at the moment, but maybe somebody will come along," no. If his planning is correct, the preparation of a harmonious situation, context or place, will attract harmony. Correct harmony follows a perfectly normal rhythmic context; call it a cosmic one, a galactic one, whatever.

The cycles of harmonious activity mesh in with each other, you can't force them, nor can you force the pace. If a thing is in harmony with a natural progression, a natural development, then it will and must harmonize; but not by being forced, not by achieving a false harmony, anymore than you can have an instrument in an orchestra tuned to a different pitch and consider it to be harmonizing. You cannot force anyone or anything into harmony. It is tuned into harmony in concert with other activities which connect to it.

■

Chapter 4

Establishing Harmony
in Individual and Group Situations

How do you build up harmony? Again, it is a similar technique to building up the capacity to relax. You don't go stamping around saying "I will harmonize with this thing" or "I will harmonize with this person or context, whatever happens."

People can and do spread themselves too thinly, if they try to harmonize with, say, everything in the world. They can also try too hard : "I'll harmonize with this thing, person, place, if it kills me." By the same token you do not choose to what circumstance, thing or place you harmonize, because there is a danger here that one will harmonize by choice : selective harmonization.You tread a careful path between "I will harmonize with everything there is" and "I will only harmonize with those things with which I want to harmonize." What you need and what you want can be different, so one initially aims to harmonize by a very simple method : we say that "like attracts like."

If a person is aiming to produce harmony in themselves, as and when they do gradually become a harmonious person within themselves, they will attract harmony from other people, from circumstances, from things. Wherever that harmony exists, they will tune into it. This development of a harmony within oneself is done through all the techniques, exercises,readings and other things within the Tradition. In the Tradition these activities are all multi-faceted : they have many effects on different levels. One of these levels is the development of harmony within oneself : if one is aiming to do this within oneself by using these activities, these mechanisms, this aim will automatically relate in concord with other harmonies which already exist.

Say one tunes into harmony, all right? Now how does one try to use this harmony at the same time as one is developing it? After all, the spin-off of developing harmony within oneself and with other situations should also be to become able to use this harmony in a decisive and useful way, both to increase the harmony of situations and to influence such situations,gatherings, or meetings in a harmonious way.

The different techniques of harmony are these : say there is a situation which you think is like the one I mentioned before when I said that harmony in its best form does not just mean the absence of disharmony, it can be at a zero point, without disharmony and without active harmony. If you want to step up the harmony, you use one of the basic tactics of the Tradition which is used to a lesser and greater extent in every area, and that is the use of energy.

Harmony itself is an energy which is being used to vibrate in harmony with other things of a cosmic or galactic nature. A particular type of harmonious energy fuels the machinery which produces and uses harmony. In a situa-tion where you detect that there is a lack of useful harmony, you can try and inject harmony into that situation by getting into the situation, harmonizing it, and trying to lift it slightly into an area of harmony.

There is always a bit of a problem here : in the course of one's effort to lift this situation onto a level of positive harmony : and not at an enormously high level, just notch by notch, step by step : one can sometimes get bogged down with such situations. You can avoid this by taking a little bit more energy to push the situation up.

Another way you can use energy to improve a situation is to influence it from the outside, i.e. without being personally involved in the situation yourself. Just as we use energy transfer from individual to individual, from individual to group, from group to individual etc., so harmony can be transmitted from an individual to a situation, from a group to a situation and so forth, because correct harmony is a positive form of energy.

There are several ways you can do this. You can look at or imagine a situation, a person or group with whom you want to harmonize or to whom you want to send a harmonizing quantity of energy, and you can concentrate on that group, having made clear your intention. It's not " Oh I think I'll think of that person, group etc.," this is imprecise, you get too wide a beam. You narrow it down, you focus it by your intention. You say to yourself what your intention is, then concentrate with a harmonious intent.

Just as we can gather together and focus the various forms of a group's energy on a situation or individual to help a person in a health or other situation, one can focus that energy on a particular aspect. If that particular aspect is harmony, one's intention calls up the type of energy which one wants to use. Don't search around and ask yourself questions like "Do have that quantity of energy?" : "Am I harmonious enough to do it?" If your intention and your decision is good enough, then that type of energy will become available, within your capacity to receive, hold, or send it.

You must be specific in these areas : not airy-fairy, not imprecise : "Oh I wish everybody would be happy" and singing and dancing and so forth. You have a technique and energy available; use it as precisely as the situation allows. You don't project what you think that the situation should develop into. If that were the case, you would already be called upon to make a sort of judgement as to how you should be working or behaving in a harmonious way. You're not stuck with such a judgement : "Oh I'd better not do it in case my judgement is wrong."

If your intention is right, and you judge that a certain situation requires the use of harmony as an energy, then fine, use it, don't try to impose the effects that such a harmony will have on that person, group or place : "I detect an atmosphere of x, y, z" : "I want everybody to be dancing with a rose in their hair" because you're then imposing conditions along with the harmony that you seek to transmit. If your intention is to contribute towards a harmonious situation, then once you've typed the energy as being of a harmonious nature, you just use it.

Also, this imposition of the type of result you want to

create by setting conditions may not work out as you have planned, which can lead to searching self-examination : "Oh I intended this to be such and such, and it wasn't. Am I wrong? Is the energy or reception wrong?" No. There can be a billisecond difference between the time you send that energy and the time it is received. You must allow the situation or the circumstance to dictate how they will use that harmonious energy in the best way. You are always a billisecond behind : by expecting the person, the place or the situation to conform exactly, you impose a limitation on the people who are receiving. It may be that things will conform exactly, there's no reason why not, at which point there's no problem. But if they don't, as long as one's intention in creating a harmonious situation is right, the energy of the harmonious intention will not be lost.

Acting in a harmonious fashion creates what one can call a magnetic flux around a person. It is not always perceptible in the sense that one goes into a situation with harmonious intent, and everybody reels back at the sight of this person stepping in with their "aura" and that sort of thing. The useful intention should be a thing which to all intents and purposes is your secret. When and as it does work, you may or may not notice it, you may or may not see it, because it may work in a way which you don't see or don't know.

It is of more benefit and use to you to make your harmonious influence felt, not secretly, but privately, than to make the "grandstand" harmony move. It's all very good and fine to say "I intend to be harmonious and you'd better believe it!" but one can behave, think, and harmoniously influence oneself, another person and a situation, more by locking into that situation or that ambiance.

If you want to take the credit for introducing harmony, well there is a story which is possibly relevant. There was a extraordinarily rich merchant in Baghdad, and throughout his life he had been quite ruthles in the pursuit of riches, and when he reached sixty, he started having misgivings. So he constructed an enormous mosque and spent an awful lot of money on it : it was with beautifully tiled with all the trimmings, and it said on it : "Sultan Muhammad built this mosque to the glory of God." When he finally died, he appeared on the day of judgement between an enormous pair of scales and everything was put on either one side or the other, and eventually the scales were just a little bit further down on the negative side, so they said "All right, take him away down below". And he said "No, just a minute, I want a recount." So they brought out the Ledger and they looked through everything he'd done, good and bad, and it was still fractionally on the down side. He said "Ah, just a minute, I didn't get credit for the mosque which I built," and they said "No, because you wrote "Sultan Muhammad built this mosque" on it : you got the credit on Earth. What you did was seen, so you don't get the credit here."

What it boils down to is this : that the intention is what makes it work. If one knows what one's intention is, and one can face and handle one's intention, then one is all right. Harmonizing does not necessarily mean homogenizing into a mass, i.e. not taking into consideration, background, race, family, etc. One harmonizes in the way one feels one is capable and able to harmonize, and this increases as one practises harmony oneself.

Some of what one might call the most primitive types of harmonizing are ways which one can call sending good or beneficial thoughts about somebody who is not present. In Arabic you mention so-and-so, and add : "May he be without problems". This may be an automatic thing to say, yet the intention is to send good wishes to somebody. In England one says : "Give so-and-so my best wishes." It may be said without thinking, but if the intention is strong and you really do mean "Give so-and-so my best wishes" rather than just mouthing it, it is a very simple way of harmonizing with that person. As Rumi says : "The intention gives birth to the act." Without intention there can be no act, and without good intention there can't be a good result.

The more you know others, the more you harmonize with them, and the more you can pick up their actions and reactions, the way they respond to your stimulus. This is only true of commercial relationships, but it holds true on different levels, whether it be in a personal, group, national, or whatever context. These are examples of how you can influence and help others in their thinking; how you can influence, help, and back up their development; how you can help them through problems, how you can start to think in certain fundamentally important areas as one entity.

You can say "This is all very well, but are we getting into the area of "Am I my brother's keeper?" No. After all, there is a degree beyond which one does not have the right or the capacity to "save a person from themselves." One is not one's brother's keeper in the sense that one is responsible for everything, and that one has to go around looking after or systematically guarding and protecting him, etc. What it does mean is that, in a group situation, if you are a part of one complex activity, anything which is beneficial reflects on the whole body politic. Anything detrimental does not infect, influence, or produce a negative effect throughout the whole system, but it does mean that the harmony which exists should be able to compensate for any negative thing.

One may not oneself be responsible for a negativity or a problem, but if a degree of harmony exists between groups, as it should between individuals, the possibility of lessening the damage, difficulty, or the tremors which spread out from a happening, can be dealt with more efficiently. You or a group can meet problems "out there" before their disturbance factor becomes great enough to produce any influence on the main setup, if you like. Where, of course, the harmony comes in is that the early-warning system operates : one has a feeling, an impression, one gathers all the little traces and little implications of thought, deed, action; one puts them all together, replays them, and one gets this so-called impression back.

I'm not only talking about negative situations but positive situations as well. One can try as an individual or as a group to push a developing positive situation forward in another group without detriment to the activities of the group which is doing the pushing; that is to say, if one is harmoniously enough associated with another group or individual, there is no sacrifice or loss of energy in sending energy, impulse, help or harmonious vibration to that other group as a tangible backup. One knows when and where and how to do this because if there is a harmonious relationship established, there will be, again, the most important factor, which is communication. One feels the tremors of negativity or positivity : if they are negative, one can get an early warning of it and take whatever actions are necessary to deal with it. If it is something positive, one can help situations to come to fruition more quickly by thought and deed than they might otherwise have done.

An individual or a group loses nothing from giving situations a push. The group or situation which is receiving it may initially consider that they have done it all by themselves. This is all right : nobody's going to say "Ha ha, we helped you" but if the groups are closely linked enough, then it is implicit that any group pulling off a successful activity will be aware of the fact tha it is highly possible that they received backup.

This should not be a source of anguish to them : "Oh why didn't they leave us alone, we could have done it by ourselves" or anything like this. It should be a simple acceptance of the fact that it is highly possible that they got backup. If they did, fine : if they didn't, it doesn't matter. They expect it, they hope for it, and they would like also to return it back into the common pool of effort, endeavor and energy.

Harmonizing on every level allows corresponding communication to pass in all directions. You're not,for goodness sake, living in each others' pockets, poking your nose into other people's affairs, wanting to know night and day what is going on with everybody else and that sort of thing : this is not harmony, this is pure nosiness. Harmony means that one thinks with, not for, other people : one harmonizes with them. Hopefully their good intentions are your good intentions, so therefore morally and with all other energy which one has at one's disposal, one backs them. It is purely a thoughtful backup : one says "Well, such-and-such a person or such-and-such a group is doing this : I hope they make it." This is an identification with the individual or with the group, and it is a beneficial thing. One hopes that one would also be on the receiving end of this.

Harmony is not something abstract : "Are we all agreed, brothers and sisters, that we are all in harmony? Yes! Well, number two on the agenda"... If that's the sort of harmony one wants, I can sit here and shout and rave and demand harmony and nobody will move a muscle. That is not then harmony, it is fear, and it is not a useful thing at all; it also creates a backlash because if you don't know what sort of harmony you're aiming for, you can overtighten the violin string. If you're tuning a piano, you either have perfect pitch or you use a tuning-fork. You cannot harmonize in a vacuum. You harmonize with something, and by definition, harmony is achieved by comparison and exchange. You have chord and discord. The two either meet, or they go off at two completely different tangents, and by definition, they can't then meet.

You can demand harmony until you're blue in the face, you can threaten that if you don't get harmony you'll do this that and the other thing, and you'll just get the same effect. What you have to do is this : you have to teach and instil into people not only the need for harmony, because you can keep on harping on it, it doesn't mean to say you get it. You instil into people how and what it is, how you can achieve it and how you should use and maintain it.

If you take it as a sort of wave of energy, harmony, by definition, must be of a positive nature, otherwise it could be a disturbance or interruption. It works on a level which can be received by another situation and meshes in with it. If both the transmitting and receiving points are reverberating on the same wavelength, then there will be no trouble in the correspondence, in the harmonious relationship. This is why you cannot dictate the reception and use of that harmonious energy or that harmonious wave. If you act in a way which you consider to be harmonious, with the intention of being harmonious, it will have a harmonious result.

In normal everyday life, one does this instinctively. If

you're going to an important meeting or a business conference, it is unusual to go in wearing a frogman's flippers and a bowler hat : one normally acts instinctively in a harmonious way. Okay, it's a surface harmony, but it's still harmony : the intention is to harmonize with other people and the situation. You then take it a step further than that : you put on the suit and whatever is required to harmonize dress-wise, appearance-wise. You're probably going to talk in a way which harmonizes with the other people, both from the point of view of the language they're using and the topic they're discussing, fine. Your intention can also be heightened by the fact that you say : "I like most of these people, so I would like to have a beneficial, cordial, elevating, interesting and amusing discussion and conversation."

That's yet another notch up in the positive of the harmonious situation. If one says "Yes but I'm going to introduce something which may be a jarring note because I'm going to have to criticize something or somebody about an activity or an area" or else "I'm plainly going to disagree with what is happening" : now how can it be that I can have all this surface harmony, being dressed right, terms of reference, language, etc., yet I'm going to introduce a note of disharmony because I have an objection or criticism? How do I equate the situation?

There are two parts to this question. Firstly, is the intention to introduce a note of disharmony purely from a disharmonious motive? i.e. "I just want to break this meeting up!" or is my intention honestly and really based on a usefully positive comment or criticism which I feel it is necessary to make for the better overall harmony of the situation, the group or the activity?

If one is properly satisfied on this basis, one says : "Okay now, in that it is possible that I will have to introduce this jarring note, I will try and increase and project my harmonious intent, so that if I have to deliver this criticism, its impact will hopefully be softened by my obvious intention that this is meant as a harmonious criticism or action, or that it is intended for the greater harmony of the group or the situation." If one has prepared the ground in a harmonious way, and from all surface and other indications the people the situation are appreciative of the fact that one's intention is indeed of a harmonious nature, then the impact will not create what one might fear, which is disharmony.

If the intention is not clear, if there is a grey area, one should be very careful about the terms of reference one uses. If these terms of reference are based on what one imagines the situation, the person or the group needs, you could be on dangerous ground, because imagination can sometimes have a lot of assumptions in it: "This thing needs a jolly good shake-up" : "Any shake-up is better than none." : "Any movement is better than no movement." This is the use of false premise.

I'm sure all of us have seen people whose claim to fame in the local pub or wherever is to say something which is either challenging, uproarious, outrageous, hostile or astonishing: not necessarily because they've had a couple of drinks too many, but because it is generally a show-off tactic. You know, the famous phrase : "Oh I don't know, I don't agree with you" and there he goes, he has latched onto an idea, he wants to have the opportunity of expounding it, he is calling attention to himself : the self-importance phenomenon. This is a gratuitously disharmonious thing, where the person hasn't thought of the long-term consequences of his actions.

One sees a lot of this sort of thing, and one might say to him later, after he's been thrown out of the saloon bar : "You know what you said last night was damn silly, wasn't it?" and he replies "I didn't think it would cause so much trouble." The operative phrase here is "I didn't think." The consequences of action can go on and on, it's the ripple effect.The intention should go together with a prognostication of the impact on the situation, as a result of what has been said.

"My intention was good." That's too imprecise for my money, as they say. If the intention is not precise, then the margin of error is much greater. "My intention was generally good." : the road to hell is paved with good intentions. What does he mean by good? Good is too abstract a connotation : Good and Evil.

So even if the intention is good, i.e. to harmonize with the situation; if the estimation of the situation you start with is incorrect or the tactic used is incorrect, no matter how harmonious the person may feel, what one must do is launch that intention of harmony, and let the other person, situation, or context take it and process it. One can try and influence a situation or a circumstance in a useful way : this has to be a judgement of one's own capacity and one's own relationship with a situation. By definition, harmony cannot be a thing which is imposed.

The intention to use and implement harmony has to be a very careful decision, that does not go to one extreme or another. First you define the intention, and then you act in such a way or do such things which, in a foreseeable way, take into consideration the person or situation and one's knowledge of the target, as it were, as far as one can see. The intention will carry the harmony through to be used.

"I think people should harmonize in this way" : the dangerous factor here is the "I think." If you say "I know," all right, but you're getting into a different ball game. If you say "I think this might work" you've already got two doubtful areas : "think" and "might." It is better to say to yourself : "My intention in involving myself with this situation is to harmonize myself with it, to do what I can in a reasonable way, and launch the harmonious energy of that intention into the target situation." Don't push it, don't predict. Make it available, and send it off.

Work out in what way you can use harmony; in what way you have already shown to yourself that you have acted, thought, or felt in a harmonious way or in a harmonious circumstance : recapture that, and use it.

In the past the word harmony has been used as too much of a throwaway. People are often not careful enough about the phrases they use : "Oh sure, harmonious development of"... Stop, just look at that. "Harmonious development" : that is a big double concept. You might say "Well, one compliments the other." One compliments the other, yes, but they can exist separately. You can have development without harmony, but the development you get without harmony is not a valuable development. You can achieve harmony, and with harmony you can achieve development : hence the concept of harmonious development is a valid one. But it is a serious and profound thing,

not a throwaway : "Gimme development and all that stuff."
No : look at it.

This kind of thinking is the equivalent of piling up
the volumes of the Mathnavi to reach a banana stashed on
top of a bookshelf. It achieves the immediate aim, which is
to get the banana, but it is not taking advantage of the
function which the Mathnavi can and does fulfil. The use of
Rumi's Mathnavi in that context is harmonious to the person's
limited and narrow aim for the moment, but to enter into its
greater harmony, it should be read.

Don't take concepts which are tangible, positive and
cosmically balanced and turn them into abstract ones. Study
them, learn how to use them, and then use them while
maintaining the capacity to understand them. That means
you don't say "Aha, I have achieved harmony. Right, what
next?" No, you keep it going all the time, without, again, the
constant reference to "Where is the harmony? It's all right,
I'll just reassure myself that it is still shipshape" because at
that point harmony doesn't become real harmony, it becomes
almost a threat : "I've got the harmony stashed here, I'll
check it to see whether rats are eating it or whether it's
getting damp" : it becomes a preoccupation about harmony.

A person like that is a professional harmonizer, and at
that point it has become a preoccupation to the exclusion
of anything else, and it is certainly not a correct use of
harmony.

The concept of harmony cannot be accumulated : you
can't accumulate real harmony without using it. So
understand it, develop it, develop the techniques for using it, and then use it.

■

Chapter 5

Individual and Group Exercises

I am sure we have all heard the familiar story of people who have taken acid or other drugs, and they say things like "The tree spoke to me." This is what is called the "false phenomenon," a poisoned state in which the various senses of hearing, touch, sight and colour have a short circuit so that people "hear" colours and things like that.

Although false, this phenomenon is a indication of the type of communication which can exist in a more enhanced state. People can say this quite normally in a non-drug situation, and it can be practiced as a normal thing. If one goes to an outdoor concert in the evening : the whole ambiance of the event is geared towards comfort and the enhanced appreciation of the music : there's nothing weird about this, it's quite normal, natural and understandable, but in the context of the Tradition, we aim not merely to require that this enhanced state be produced by ambiance or lighting and colour effects, but that it should be a sort of mobile scenario.

This means that one can recreate that ambiance within oneself as a result of having understood and appreciated what that ambiance creates within one. You don't necessarily have to go to a particular place to appreciate a particular piece of music : supposing one has gone several times to the outdoor place and heard the concert, it's perfectly possible to recapture the ambiance and get a heightened appreciation of that particular piece of music by listening to that concert on a gramophone record. If one can do that, then either in a group exercise or individually, one can start each exercise on the same or on a higher level, without going through every lower stage over and over again in order to achieve it. One slots in as near as possible to where one left off the last time.

43

That is not to say that certain activities and exercises are not better done in a particular ambiance. There are certain hot spots or places where things are much more highly charged, and the amount of feedback is therefore that much greater. You have places or situations where teachers, performance, the colour, lighting and other things enhance the situation and improve the benefit and the rapport with the activity. There are situations where all these factors come together : the place, the colour, the arrangement, the event and the people. These things all build up, and as one learns the various functions of places, people, colour, sound, and other tactics, one can recreate in one's memory the actual and tangible influence of those specific things, and one should indeed attempt to recreate them.

One can say "Yes, but of course there is the time factor. Very true, I have said before that no activity is always the same, because the time factor always changes it : but if that time factor is going along with the activity, which it is, then there's no problem. One shouldn't say "Ah yes, but that was then and this is now" : if one is in tune and in harmony with the activity, then it will develop along with the time factor.

But don't try to recapture every minute aspect of an experience, in every possible detail. This can be an end in itself : one says "Okay, at such-and-such a time I went to such-and-such a place" and then one starts filling in all the gaps; "What was the colour of the place, what was there, who was there, what were they wearing, where was I sitting" : by the time one has filled in as many of the gaps as possible, it's the next day. There is a point beyond which the remembering or the recreation of a situation or ambiance is complete enough to start doing something. One doesn't have to go through every infinitely detailed aspect of it to remember it, unless one is specifically asked to do so.

When I talk about recreating circumstances, I mean a recreation up to the point where it becomes familiar enough to use as a point of departure for doing an exercise, listening to music, or doing whatever is necessary. One prepares the ground in as reasonable a way as one can, without it becoming an activity in itself. It's part of the preparatory period before doing something.

Otherwise, not only can it become an end in itself: filling in all the gaps, dotting your i's, crossing your t's; but an element of exasperation can also creep in: "I don't remember this little factor, or that feature, or was the ashtray on the left or the right, or was I wearing this or that?" No, if your focus is overly detailed, then the thing goes off. It's a familiar phenomenon, and it is part of a negative sabotage and escape factor which is always present.

When I talk about the negative, don't forget it's not this terrible threat of "The negative will get you". The negative is a sort of sly, lazy part of the character. If it has the opportunity of distracting your attention from anything positive, with a very slight movement, with a very slight change of direction, it will do so. Its menace is not of a strong nature, it is by default that persons give in to their own inner tension, laziness, impatience or whatever, and allow the negative to then direct them in an erroneous direction. This direction is not necessarily disastrous. It can be in a stupid direction, which will increase their impatience. Then they will realize that they have been impatient at a particular time and become impatient with themselves for having become impatient, and therefore you get an algebraic permutation.

The question here is how to concentrate one's attention and energies in an activity or in an exercise, capitalizing on all possible positive streams of energy and influences which exist. There is a terrible transatlantic term: "maximizing" and that is precisely what we're really talking about. In a way, maximizing means remembering carefully: it is a familiar exercise.

There is another familiar kind of maximizing effort, which is, "I will recreate all the things which I remember to have been functional in a given circumstance, and I will attempt to apply them all." One then ends up in possibly the same stew as before: "How do I use this?", "What do I know?" etc. There's over-maximizing as well: "Oh I should be able to do that" : "I should be able to" or "I would like to be able to" can be two different things.

Sufism for Today

You maximize by recollection of the segments which one can reasonably remember and apply within what one considers to be one's own competence, and without picking and choosing. If one brings these segments together, the ones which one can reasonably, usefully and functionally apply will relate to each other. The other segments which are slightly outside, or which one can't immediately relate and use, should not be forced into a pattern : they will harmonize if they are supposed to, if they can, and if you can help them. Never force them, never pressure them into use. The harmonizing influences of a situation inevitably form their own pattern. You cannot keep them apart, you can't force them together. They homogenize in a natural way : their function is to do so.

Your function is to try and recollect them, hold them together, and then interact with them as part of the pattern. They are not using you, you are not using them, you are becoming part of the pattern with them. If one can allow oneself to be less preconceived-notion and pattern-minded, it helps. Terms of reference are important. Say one has, by inclination, conditioning or background, considered x object, x colour, to be good, bad, indifferent, "my" colour, "his" colour, "their" colour etc., one is then sort of stuck with it. This can be a stumbling block.

For instance, I come from a mountain people : I assure you, I get seasick in my bath. I can't stand the sea, I think it's an unnatural, reprehensible thing. However, if I considered, for instance, that the sea is green and therefore "I dislike green," I would have a problem, because I am also born a Muslim and one of the Prophet's banners was green. I could consider green as anathema, and it would be a problem, or else it's "I love green" and therefore by definition "I must love the sea" : I would then have a tug-of-war within myself. So, predetermined, preconceived, conditioned points of view or attitudes can be stumbling-blocks within the Tradition.

There is very little contradiction within the Tradition with what one might call normal reasonable attitudes, values, politeness, consideration, or intelligence. One will very

46

rarely, if ever, find oneself faced with a choice between doing something polite which is demanded by society, and behaving in a way in the Tradition which would be incorrect according to those circumstances. There is really no collision.

Since there is no collision, what one has to do is detach oneself so that, say one is listening to some music, as "music from within the Tradition. " Okay, at the back of one's mind, if one is musically-minded, you may consider some of it off-key or even cacophonous, but nobody's forcing you to suspend your judgement entirely, forcing you to listen to a lot of dervishes beating old tin kettles with you being obliged to smile and think how beautiful and sanctified it all is. No, one will feel : "Well it's a bit weird, but I dunno" : one isn't being asked to judge it in comparison to Elgar or Bach. So there is a certain suspension of one's conventional judgement and terms of reference, but there should be no confrontation.

Confrontation is like oppression, dictatorship, force or tension : an unnatural circumstance. It occurs very occasionally, but it shouldn't happen as a regular thing. There should be no traumatic situations where one is torn between this or that, so to speak. If a situation like that does come up, it can and should be examined from a detached point of view, on the assumption, I am sorry to say, that if there is any confusion, one mght be in error. Possibly one is trying to bend one thing to take on the form of another thing, which implies tension, pressure. If there is such a collision, misunderstanding or contradiction, I think that one should first look at one's own point of view, motivation, hang-ups, conditioning, before either blaming what one thinks one should do within the Tradition or what society is imposing on one.

It's not the mea culpa syndrome "I am always wrong." No, it is allowing for the fact that laziness of thought, greediness, imprecision or whatever negative failing or weakness one has will manifest itself. It's Murphy's Law : if there is a possibility of doing something stupid, the likelihood is that one will do it. This is an unfortunate thing, and if one recognizes it, then one can analyze it, look at it, and benefit from it.

Examine the situation as dispassionately as possible in a gentle way, and see what happened, what produced a state around oneself and within oneself in order to communicate with people and the circumstances in this way : all the while keeping firmly in mind what one is trying to do, what one's intention is. If one keeps that in mind, that is the compass-point, the star, if you like, by which one steers. Then during the course of an exercise or an activity, if one's attention wanders off, it can be brought back into focus, or back onto the direction of one's intention. If one hasn't clearly defined one's intention before beginning, then it's very possible that one's attention can be distracted during an activity and focused on something seemingly interesting, valuable or fascinating, and at that point you get what we call the "butterfly mind" : you hop around.

There is a direction, an intention, and one goes for it calmly and dispassionately : not "despite everything" because when you're doing that, it implies tension. Don't wallow, don't wander : take the short cuts. There are short cuts, i.e. activities or exercises of different natures which enhance the experience or the person's ability to take advantage of certain energies. These short cuts are not used system-atically one after another, over and over again, because there would then be nothing but short cuts : but if the ob-ject is to go from A to B, why not use them?

The short cuts that exist in the Tradition are indicated in a way which is specific to individuals. It is only very occasionally that a short cut will be indicated to a whole group, because a group after all is composed of individuals. It is usually the case that one will decide that a person doesn't need to go from a to b this way round, and that they can short cut an exercise or an experience by a particular activity that will be specific to them. This is one of the reasons why, as you go along, you will find you should avoid what I call the "doctor's waiting room syndrome" like the plague. That is when you have a bunch of people sitting outside in the doctor's waiting room, and somebody comes out and somebody says "What did he give you?" and

Individual and Group Exercises

he says "Streptomycin" and everybody goes out and buys Streptomycin although one of them has a broken leg, just because it's been given to one of the other patients.

If there is a group activity or exercise, or an exercise which can be done independently of the group, this is fine, it is common knowledge. If there's a particular activity, exercise, action or piece of reading given specifically to the person, they should keep it to themselves. It's not secrecy in the sense of "I've got a secret" : it is a particular and personal thing which other people don't need to know, either because it might confuse them, or because they might do it. This would not lead to any terrible accident or difficulty, but since it doesn't apply to them, it wouldn't be useful or productive. At worst it might be confusing, and who needs any more confusion?

You fix on an activity with your intention. Such fixing does not imply a rigidity, an inflexibility. Fix one's intent on something, yes, but with what they call "calm purpose." Not "I have to do it, in case..." No, one knows how to do it, one is required to do it, which is useful; and, given the intention, if one puts it together with the required energy, one can carry it out.

No requirement made by a teacher on a person or group will be more than they are able to do : that is, it will not be an impossible task : it requires a little bit of normal and useful effort. It's never just there; it's always just a little further off, so at least a minimum effort has to be made. What has to be judged by the person who is doing the teaching is that the person is capable of doing whatever it is for the purpose of acquiring energy, or for whatever they are capable of doing.

This is common sense in any case, because there is nothing more disheartening for people than to be given a number of things to do, and then be unable to do it : they then turn on themselves as being incapable, or turn on the Tradition for not being coherent enough. So the activities which are given are just slightly beyond the person's experience but not out of range of the person's capacity.

One should always extend, reach upwards. It's always

49

easier to reach downwards : if one reaches upwards it is slightly more taxing, but if the aim of the target is within one's capacity, it can be in one's grasp. This is as it should be, because there is nothing useful in aspiring to something which is unattainable and regularly falling short.

■

Chapter 6

Group Organization and Change

All of you together in a meeting produce harmony and an energy. You pass it among yourselves and you share it. When you go home, you don't put that harmony and energy in a drawer and leave it inside for another year. You have worked hard for this harmony and energy, so it is only correct that you use it correctly. When you leave a meeting, you take with you certain mental pictures as well as the memory of the feeling, of the ambiance. Use these two factors, the visual memory and the memory of the feeling, to remind you of the harmony you have experienced during the year to come.

· There are always times during a year when a person or a group may feel a little bit low, a little bit down. It is especially at moments like this that you take hold. It's not like taking an aspirin if you have a headache in order to make it go away : it is reminding yourself of a harmony, of an ambiance that has taken place, and, at a time when one might feel lonely or down, re-experiencing that feeling of harmony. It is not putting yourself back in time, it is putting yourself forward in experience.

The feeling of harmony is an actual reality, not an abstract concept, because it is something you can and should and do use. If you are in harmony with the previously experienced harmony, that will tell you when and how to use it. Harmony takes many forms : politeness and consideration for other people is a form of harmony, and increases harmony. If you think about other people's comfort and other people's well-being, you are harmonizing with those people, and it is also a positive factor producing positive energy.

For the benefit of friends who are with us for the first time : one's reaction to an initial meeting can be a bit confusing

51

because one is impacted upon in various ways and from various directions, and if one analyzes these impacts from a surface or conditioned point of view, some may appear contradictory, and one then tries to come up with an explanation using conventional judgement.

You cannot arrive at a correct judgement of the unconventional by using conventional measurements. It is worse still is if there is no obvious explanation and you try to force an explanation on yourself : this is guaranteed to cause confusion or add to it. So what is the attitude or technique to take up in a situation like this? In a way the answer is conventional, but it is also practical and harmoniously useful. Observe. Experience. Listen. Think.

Think, don't worry. Don't say : "I haven't understood this today, what can I do?" "Everybody else seems to have understood, what is the matter with me?" There are things every day or every week or every year which I say to you, some of which you will understand now, some of which you will understand in a week, in a month, in a year or in ten years, but you will understand them. This is a promise, not a threat.

Use the senses which God has given you. You feel, you observe, you think, you walk, you experience : you do not have to decide every night before you go to sleep whether you have understood what has happened during the day : this is an unrealistic and non-functional target to set yourselves.

Another very real question is that of communication, which can be a very real problem. Think all the time how to increase communication. Don't preoccupy yourself constantly with this idea, but always be alert to the possibility of increasing communication.

When communication breaks down, there should always be an alternative. If the communication depends on electricity and the electricity is cut, you should always have a fail-safe, an alternative. This aspect of having an alternative communication relates directly to the exchange of energy between people and the Tradition. Between individual people and the Tradition there are hundreds and thousands of different ways of communicating, and in no way and at no time can this communication be totally interrupted. As I have said before, believe it and practice it : the more you practice it, the more familiar and able you are to use it.

In any situation where there is an interior or a personal problem : don't look at it in isolation. There are very few interior problems which really are in isolation. They all have a connection with something. Look at the problem from the point of view that "I am looking at this problem with the assistance and energy of the Tradition, it is not just me in isolation looking at this problem in isolation." The connection with the energy of the Tradition is your savings, but you must use it. Not because if you don't use it you lose it, but the more regularly you use the contact and energy, the more familiar it becomes to you.

You don't get worried about things like : "Should I use it? Can I use it? Am I taking it from somebody else?" No. If you really feel and have really examined a situation, and it doesn't have to always be a problem situation : I have just taken a problem as an example : in any situation, look at it, examine the situation, and then feel : judge. If you feel and judge that it is correct, then connect with the energy. If your judgement or feeling has been wrong, there is no problem. If your judgement has been right, you get the extra push or whatever is needed.

So you judge, you make decisions which you feel that you have the knowledge or the capacity to make. You make your intention clear to yourself : you have a short and reasonable debate with yourself. When I say "short" I mean it, otherwise the discussion between yourself and your other self goes on, and the decision is being put off, and when and if you finally make a decision, it is possible by then that you have forgotten what the problem was.

Judging or measuring or deciding is a tactic and a technique which you learn how to apply to yourself. If you know that your decisions are usually based on either one thing or another, then you can look at this decision physically. I am talking about important decisions, I am not talking about average decisions. Each person has a priority list of decisions. Sometimes the priorities change a little bit. Circumstances change, and the time always changes. The critical thing in decision-making is the time factor.

Time is a funny thing; it can be stretched, it can be compressed. The clock turns, the calendar changes, but I am not talking about that sort of time : I am talking about the interior time. Interior time can be stopped or stretched or compressed. It can be stretched or expanded in a situation which really requires more time. The human being is following our minute and day time factor; but inside that exterior time factor is the inner time factor.

If you are reading something or doing something within the context of the Tradition, and you are doing it in the correct way and with the correct intention, interiorly you can stretch the time until you have enough time to do it. This is a little bit complicated : you can say that in exterior time you are following a clock or a calendar, but your interior time or interior development is not dependant upon that calendar or clock. Nature has decreed that people will have enough time to complete an activity. "How much? How long? Which activity? Which activity is better?" This you learn by experience, not by reading it in a book.

To sum it all up : from time to time make it a little bit of an additional exercise. Examine the situation, examine what you might call your decision-making process patiently and objectively, not in a hostile or critical fashion, i.e. that "I will find something wrong" because then you certainly will. Again, if you say "I'll have a look at that, but I'm sure there's nothing wrong" then you won't find anything.

You look towards it saying "I think there might be something good or something bad. If I find something which is not correct, I will not be horrified, I will look at it and try to do something about it. If I find something or some things which are good and positive, than I will be content and happy about it, but I won't stand there for days and days looking at it and saying : "How nice they are, I am so marvellous!"

Self-examination is an objective and patient and sympathetic activity. It is a slow activity; if you don't do it patiently, you get impatient. If it is not objective, then what you discover or what you find will not be the objective reality. If it is not sympathetic, then parts of you will close off to this inspector who is looking for something.

If your intention towards yourself is a correct one, you are using your correct activity as a contact to the energy, to the Tradition : you must constantly try to use and keep that contact. You don't say, again, in isolation : "There is the contact, I will put it on the mantelpiece and occasionally look at it" because in that way it gathers dust and becomes an object of veneration or superstition, and as time passes, you or your children or friends might forget what it actually means.

Somebody asked me two or three months ago : "Why is it among the Sufis or in Islam that you don't have the equivalent gesture of the cross?" The answer, of course, is that we see no reason to constantly recall an instrument of torture; and the second very good reason is : "You want the cross, you keep it, we have Jesus."

In order to function efficiently a group must have a structure, but when creating a structure, it should not become a monolith, otherwise you have something like a government ministry. Over the years the ministry develops other div-isions, and sub-divisions and sub-divisions of sub-divisions, and eventually you get a situation where a person going to that ministry can't find his way through it, or can't find a person who will help him with what he needs. So when I talk about making small sub-groups within a Group, I'm not talking about building a monolith or a bureaucracy.

As a group and as individuals, a group in the Tradition must function harmoniously. The energy generated by the group is circulated among the individuals who compose the group, and if an individual is functioning correctly, he or she will receive the energy and pass on a proportion of it to another person. That person shouldn't hold onto the energy and just keep it without knowing how to use it or how to pass it on, because if this happens, the flow and use of that energy becomes interrupted. I'm sure you have all from time to time been into a government office and seen a man sitting at a desk with a pile of files a foot high. That man is, in effect, stopping the action of government, stopping the flow of energy.

When a group becomes large enough, and is working harmoniously enough together and relating to other groups; certain sub-functions of the group should be established at that time. In every group we have people who discharge the function of Murshid or Murshida. They are usually people who have been longer in the group and have more knowledge and information about the Tradition. Part of their function, as far as their knowledge goes, is to explain certain aspects of the Tradition to newer members; to make themselves available, possibly to establish and sit in on small discussion groups, to generally explain and help the correct functioning of a Group, and to explain certain exercises and technical terms which we use in the Tradition.

As a group starts functioning more coherently, the almost-vague position of Murshids or Murshidas should be made clearer. Specific areas of responsibility are suggested to them. Having noted their particular or personal interests or capacities, they are encouraged to use them within the context of the Tradition.

The value or the importance of a group is not judged by the number of people in the group, nor by the number of Murshids or Murshidas that it has. The Naib is not judged by how many or how few Murshids or Murshidas, or indeed members, are in the group. The only judgement I employ when looking at a group is the quality of their effort. The sole measure I use in putting a person in a position of responsibility is their ability to function in that position. I have no favorites, and I use no emotional judgement in these areas.

The energy produced by a group is directly proportional to the amount of real effort which they put in to their activities. As to the degree of effort they have put in: a group should aim at a certain constant level of effort. The Tradition does and must work in a harmonious and balanced way. Equilibrium and harmony mean just that. Harmony cannot be of a stop-start variety.

Another reason I introduce certain modifications of

activity is because of the changing circumstances which apply to the world outside. The Tradition does not react to outside influence, but since the Tradition and the people who compose the Tradition live and work in the world outside, and since the character and nature of the Tradition is above all developmental, although the Tradition will not be subject to pressures from outside, nevertheless tactics and techniques within the Tradition can be modified to take into consideration things which have developed outside.

In no way can, and at no time has, the Tradition compromised on its basic values. There is a very considerable and very important difference between modification and compromise : modification and flexibility give a strength. As an example, supposing this, (Holds a pencil, resting its base on the table) is a point of extreme importance, one of the values of the Tradition. If the base is stable, this is modification. (Moves pencil while holding its point on the same place) This is compromise.(Waves whole pencil around the table) So, functionally and technically, there is an enormous difference between these two factors.

No teacher in the Tradition has ever had the authority to compromise with the basic values of the Tradition. The enormous flexibility of the Tradition, in any case, makes any sort of compromise unnecessary. You can take the blade on a fine damascene sword, and bend it from the point to the hilt : that same sword will cut through steel. Salman i-Farsi wrote that when the snow falls, the branch of the cherry tree bows beneath the weight of the snow, and it sleeps in the winter beneath the blanket of snow. In the heat of the sun of the spring, the snow melts and the branch takes up its original position. It could have remained and held its rigidity, and broken : its function is to survive and produce cherries the next year, not to prove its courage against the elements.

From time to time those of us who are charged with looking after the Tradition in various parts of the Universe have to look far ahead, not only to see how the Tradition is functioning among its people, but also to clearly and positively predict what modifications may be necessary. This is not merely technical updating : just as teachers in the Middle Ages would send messengers by horse or camel with their orders, so I naturally use a telephone, fax or cassette because it is efficient and useful to do so. No great examination or prediction of the future is necessary to take advantage of technological advance.

When I say we look far into the future and we predict, I am not talking about "Madame Fifi and her crystal ball." In looking ahead and planning the techniques of the Tradition for the future, we greatly benefit from similar work which has been done by past teachers, who have either left specific and detailed indications of what should be done, or who have indicated that at the beginning of a certain time, consideration should be given to certain specific things : for instance that at a given time, one should study and consider a certain evolutionary change, measure it when you feel that it is coming, and build in and modify the Tradition in line with that evolution.

This drops a whole load of responsibility on a teacher who, with respect to those notes from the past, finds himself in the situation where he has to initiate certain new activities. He has received a polished and functioning instrument : he must also keep it polished and functioning in his own time so that he can hand it on in the same state. For approximately the last seven years I have been studying and considering one recent aspect for us in terms of the Tradition, and that is the new situation and condition of women in the present-day world. I'm not saying I've been thinking about and working on it for seven years because women have been present among us for only that time; it means that I am dovetailing this in with tactics, techniques and suggestions which in a way terminated seven years ago.

This area of study is not provoked because of the upsurge of feminism. The need for techniques and modifications are produced by a number of factors. I'll mention some, not in order of importance or priority : women are increasingly taking up their correct and proportionate place in the world; in commercial, political, medical and all other areas of activity. In case anybody hasn't noticed there are a very large number of women and it is normal that such a large proportion of the population of the world should become involved in every function of society. You might say "Well, this is not particularly new, it is a natural ongoing situation" and "Should this affect or influence women in general, or women in the Tradition in particular?"

Again, one or two examples; not necessarily in order of importance : as women take on more and different jobs and responsibilities, they are becoming subject to more and more pressures and tensions in which they could be genetically vulnerable. Now if that sounds threatening, ominous or menacing, it is not.

The whole population of the world is being subjected to more and more tensions and pressures. When I say that one can predict that women are more genetically vulnerable, it doesn't mean to say that they are more weak or faulty : it means that they can be vulnerable because they are, in fact, more sensitive than men. They are more prescient than the average man, therefore the impact of sustained pressures and tensions are likely to affect them more than it affects men.

Looking ahead several years or generations, it is possible that participation of women in world affairs might even diminish, because of the buildup of tension and pressures over the years and generations. If the statistics start to show that a significant number of women are falling ill, women's own enthusiasm for full participation will either diminish, or else society might say : "Women can't stand the increasing pace of life."

Other factors can affect this picture, as well. One can foresee that social or medical influences will be able to help women to overcome these difficulties. It is possible that certain elements of pressure or tension which exist at the moment will diminish. I'm not going to express an opinion that I think they will diminish or whether psychologists or medical science will develop an answer.

One function of my research has been to study this question so, that if the black picture of tension and pressure I have painted above does happen, I should have left my instructions or opinions as to how a situation like that could be handled : in other words how women in the Tradition and how the families who are in immediate contact with them can be supported or sustained. This implies a number of modifications in technique.

Such a technique could be aimed at making women as stupid and insensitive as men so that they wouldn't suffer, but I don't think that is a very evolutionary and developmental concept. What is actually much simpler than making women stupid is to modify tactics and techniques in the Tradition in ways that have always been done under similar circumstances, i.e. in such a way that nothing significantly changes except for giving the women in the various groups a feeling and sense of optimism, so that they don't feel they are ignored or that their needs are not also served in the Tradition.

I have said before that for many years and generations the Tradition was considered a sort of male-dominated men's private club. I also said that in the Tradition we have had women saints. I also pointed out that, proportionate to their number, the number of women teachers in the Tradition has been very small.

I also pointed out that one of the reasons is : what are the required qualities and nature of a teacher? My answer was that some of the characteristics required of a teacher do not come easily to women in general. For instance the capacity to be cold, dispassionate, clinical in certain situations, and not to allow any subjective emotion to cloud their judgement, and to be able, if necessary, to maintain a cold or even callous face to people they are teaching. These aspects of a nature are generally foreign to the makeup of a woman.

This is all the more difficult because such qualities have to be learned by a teacher. It makes it difficult, because you might say "Well I know a woman who has a heart of stone; she'd make a marvellous teacher." Such a male or female is the last person to do this. The person who makes the best teacher has a warm heart, which, under necessary circumstances, he or she can switch off. That is a comment just by the side, and partly explains why women teachers, and the number of women who have written great works in the Tradition, is proportionately small.

In the Tradition, we can, do, and must look after our own. Any modification, adaptation, upheaval or other thing which may occur has to be what we call "fed into" the technique of the system. It must harmonize with the situation, so that's why I say : don't think of or expect some sort of dramatic change of direction or emphasis. I need your cooperation, and when the time comes to introduce such modifications as will be necessary, I will make any modifications quite clear to avoid any sort of confusion. If such modifications or changes of emphasis are introduced, please do not rush to the nearest telephone to phone a friend in another group to see whether their modifications are better than your modifications.

Regarding discipline within the Tradition : in some cultures, when you use the word "discipline" this evokes a certain sentiment. When they hear the word discipline some people think of a rigid, blind, obedient marionette. I want to speak of a discipline which is as far as possible away from that image. We do demand a certain discipline of the people who are in the Tradition. There is an organization and people are supposed to behave in a disciplined way. Orders are passed on and carried out, and activities are directed. Authority is delegated to certain people and their instructions are carried out, otherwise you would obviously have chaos.

The other forms of discipline are the disciplines which people in the Tradition impose on themselves. In the physical body, the different systems like respiration, blood circulation etc., work in a disciplined fashion and compliment each other. There is no competition between the respiratory and the circulatory system. If there was, you would have a recipe for chaos, and the result would be illness.

Everybody accepts the fact that these various systems work together harmoniously. However in less well-defined areas the picture is unfortunately different : you have a combination of intellect fighting with identity and personality. A very usual reaction from a western person when you say "you will enter into a form of discipline" is to receive an answer : "But what about my identity or my personality?" In the Tradition, the personality has no particular value. Nobody is saying that a person enters into the Tradition and loses this highly esteemed personality or identity. If anything, the identity or personality of a person becomes clearer in the Tradition. "I will not subordinate my identity to a discipline" : it is not that this famous identity is so important, it is that they don't understand what discipline they are being asked to produce. Just as disciplined thought produces disciplined action, so an interior discipline imposed on oneself produces a deep effect.

There is a well-used measure to judge whether a person is thinking in a disciplined fashion or not, and that is to invite questions. I do this frequently when I say "If you have a question, I will be available. Construct the question, ask me." Over the years people have thought that I am either mad or a masochist to make such an open invitation. I am neither one nor the other : without giving away any of the secrets of the way I operate, sometimes I invite questions so that people can just "get something out" which is inside them. Sometimes when I listen to their questions, I am profiting from that time to think about something else. I am conscious of the tone of their questions, and therefore I am alert, I'm not ignoring their questions. Sometimes I am measuring their thought-discipline by the way in which they have formed a disciplined question.

A disciplined question reflects a disciplined thought-process. I do not spend my time entering into your minds to discipline your thoughts; I can and I do systematically indicate to you how to think in a disciplined way. I explain how discipline functions in order that you should try and carry out that discipline and benefit from the result. I benefit from people thinking in a disciplined fashion : when I see it happening, this satisfies my professional being.

When I see that it is not happening correctly, I consistently try and make corrections. I feed out the technique to be taken up and used; I go on doing this over and over again, and I modify and amend my techniques almost interminably : but again, I cannot think for you. It is not difficult to impose discipline on a group. A sheepdog does not find it very difficult to impose discipline on a flock of sheep. I have no intention of being a sheepdog : whether you want to be sheep or not is your own choice.

This is not a long drawn out complaint. It is to remind you of a very critical factor of the Tradition : a considerable degree of the discipline is self-imposed. You are present with yourselves all the time; you have the opportunity to correct yourselves with the knowledge, hopefully, of why you correct yourself; not criticizing and chasing yourselves all the time but accepting the fact that you hope you know what is good for yourself. Unless you are basically motivated by this desire to develop yourselves, neither I nor anybody else can impose such a discipline on you.

If you believe that development is worthwhile, then you must accept the necessity of imposing self-discipline on yourselves. This discipline is not an abstract entity. If you are supposed to do a particular zikr or a particular exercise, you impose the discipline to do this upon yourself. If you are looking for, or finding an excuse not to do what's necessary, it should be your self-discipline which makes you do it.

That discipline should not take the form of shouting at yourself to do it, nor should it cajole or persuade you to do it. It should be a clear recognition of the fact that one should be doing something : by doing it you are obeying a discipline and you are discharging a responsibility towards yourself. You do it, not because you're afraid that your teacher will punish you for not doing something; there's no question of punishment : you're just not getting the result that you need.

Disciplining yourself to accept participation in a particular group activity is also important. You do it because you have persuaded yourself by discipline that it is necessary. If you can persuade yourself that it is not necessary or valuable, you are not using your self-discipline.

You might say that he talks a lot about discipline because he is a soldier, and soldiers are well-known for esteeming discipline above all things. Let me say to you that, both in that context and as a teacher, I have seen the value of discipline, and I assure you I have looked at both situations very clearly, both as a soldier and as a teacher. I have stars on my shoulder and not in my eyes.

A soldier obeys the command of his superior officer immediately. An officer says to a soldier "Now, you, when I say go, you go." If he is a good officer he chooses the right soldier, and he knows that when he says "go" the soldier will go in a thinking fashion, and that it is a trained soldier he is telling to go. Therefore, because of his training and discipline, this soldier doesn't stand up, look around, scratch his head, and wander off in that general direction. If he does so, he gets his head shot off.

One might say "Well that is the fault of the officer who chose him and told him go" : it would be the fault of the officer if he'd just chosen anybody at random. But if he knows that the soldier has been trained to work in a battle context, that he will go forward, keep his head down and not get his head shot off; assuming he is trained and properly disciplined, say the officer gives the order to go and the soldier goes; the officer can survey the progress of that soldier, but the responsibility of how he carries out his orders is on the trained soldier.

During the battle, the officer can direct him, help him, and try and influence the situation; but the officer cannot be expected to stand up and say : "A little bit to the left, down on the right, keep your head down, hold your gun up!" The officer has the right to expect the soldier to act in the way he has been properly trained to do. And the soldier has a right to expect that the officer knows what he is doing.

Training within the Tradition has very distinct steps. For instance it demands a suspension of impatience : the knowledge, the information and energy which is necessary to a person comes at the right time. If one has a tendency towards impatience, this tendency should be disciplined, which does not mean being suppressed. If one thinks, one wants to know more or advance more quickly. The disciplined question is : "Can I, at the moment, use more information? Or can I usefully advance more quickly?"

My function is to push, and not hold back. On occasions I wonder whether this very clear fact is understood. The more information, the more energy I can give out, the better

Group Organization and Change

I am functioning, but I cannot be persuaded or cajoled into giving something out when the time is not right.

When I talk about self-discipline I'm not recommending an enormous and weighty self-examination, because this in itself can be self-defeating. If a person is thinking in a disciplined fashion, the next area of activity or thought will indicate itself.

Like attracts like, positive attracts positive; and discipline should not be confused with domination or control. Discipline is the discipline of thought, and discipline of behaviour is harmonizing with the situation. Occasionally from time to time, take aspects of the Tradition like discipline or other tactics and relate yourselves to them. Make them familiar to yourself, and harmonize these aspects with each other.

■

Chapter 7

Evaluating Situations and their Abuse

Someone recently asked me who a "non-person" might be
They would be an evil intentioned cultist, dictator or politician
If a person who has one positive element within oppresses
another, his or her own stature in a positive sense diminishes
by one. If they do the same to two people, each of whom have
one positive element, their stature or positive quotient will be
diminished by two. The more people they do it to, the more
their stature or possibility diminishes because there's a minus
factor that also applies : i.e. the lower you are, the lower you'll
go. Thus their relationship with direct harmony, order, and
their own being is in a minus relationship to the positive. Do
they have to work harder to make up for that? The answer is
no, because when they lose it, they lose it. They are what is
known as honour losers.

The reason for this is that if you disturb something within
an ordered cosmological system, the order and balance doesn't
like being disequilibrated, so it reacts very strongly, quickly
and directly, not at the so-called system which is being set up,
sniping off the outposts, cutting it down, no. It hits the root, and
this root is nearly always the political, money and other social
structures which support and encourage the system. If you cut
those off, the plant falls down, because it has no validity within
the galactic balance. It's a fungus : if you cut off the nourish-
ment of a fungus which depends on a negative artificial fuel
like fear, it will topple. Such people do get wiped out, but you
see, they don't carry the entire responsibility as beings for
having done a particular thing : so you can say "They are in hell
and damnation and fire and brimstone" etc., but this is not true,
it's too simplistic. They become examples : people hopefully
learn from them.

The bigger they are the harder they fall, because they

construct a pyramid based on an artificial power-structure. This means that not only do they fall at the apex, but the pyramid which has supported them, i.e. whatever portion of society or humanity supporting them, also suffers. Maybe they will suffer to a lesser extent because the degree of shock is attenuated, but it still is there in the form of example, and people should learn from very simple things, which are the examples of history.

A negative force or system consumes itself; it must. This is categorical. It's not a question of "I hope it must," because it is only made up of the negative : it is based on contempt for the human being. For all its weaknesses, aberrations, stupidities, laziness, implausibilities and so on, the human being yet has a place. To not only ignore its place but to debase it is the thing which cannot be done. You can kill millions, people have done and do so, but it is not possible to go on doing so in the long run. It threatens a disequilibrium, and imbalance is contrary to galactic law to any significant extent, so it's just a question of time. If you build contempt for a human being, it produces contempt of human conditions, contempt for life, death and suffering : these things are then imposed by fear, harassment, torture and whatever; arrogance and manipulation and so forth come in and what you are doing is building on an insolid foundation.

Now this is a sweeping generalization, but occasionally I indulge in the luxury of such things : in the Soviet Union, you have what is basically a peasant people. By upbringing, experience and other things, they tend to be slower to reaction because their behavioral patterns are geared to things like seasons, like plants : they are therefore slower to react as a body of people. During the Soviet revolution and after, the so-called aristocracy and intelligentsia were consistently, brutally and ruthlessly butchered or thrown out by the Soviet system. Those who reacted were either killed or put aside, and the people who were brought in to fill the gaps were unable to do so. The stresses and terror built up within society because the situation was that they were trying to get a child to do a man's job without the knowledge, without the context, without the fabric.

You take the best harvester from Nitsuperkosk or some

where and you make him chief of agriculture of whatever region: he's not going to be able to do anything. He is conscious of his limitations and is also afraid, therefore this will inevitably lead to disaster. You can't ask people to do more than they are capable of doing.

So they will slowly, themselves, develop. Why the satellite countries are sort of continually steaming is that the intelligentsia were so ruthlessly destroyed as they were in the Soviet Union. Therefore it is an absolute inevitability, they must react: they're not beasts of the field. You can beat them more than you might beat an aristocrat but eventually he hurts the same, and he's going to get up and say "Enough!"

The whole purpose of being in tune or aware of situations is to be able to take advantage of them. People do this naturally. They go out in the morning, they feel cold, go back in again, put on a sweater and go out. This is a natural thing, it is no big deal. Hopefully, they don't have to sit down and work it all out esoterically, psychoanalytically, or any other way, it's a natural reaction to a circumstance. There are of course areas where one has to employ more sophisticated terms of reference, or ask advice. Again you have the two extremes to be avoided; you go out, it's raining; you don't therefore indulge in a vast "circumstance assimilation." No, if you are using your common sense, it tells you to get an umbrella. You do not employ an umbrella in a context where you need to work something out or employ more sophisticated terms of reference.

Yet people do these things, and it causes confusion, hostility and friction. Sometimes it can be because two people react to a particular situation in different ways, and when they part and go off, they may look at the situation and try and work out what it means and come up with two different explanations and identify one or the other attitude as being hostile, dictatorial or something like that. This applies to five, six, ten, fifty, a hundred people: unfortunately you can have twenty-five or forty-five different so-called understandings of a situation. What is the common understanding that they should all be taking from that situation? The answer to that is usually that they should not go away and analyze it to pieces, right down to the last component. They have already recorded some of the value or necessity of that situation, but if they are over-sophisticating it, they will very often reject what they themselves have felt and say "Oh, that's too simple" or "Maybe there's something else" or "I should dig deeper."

Now there are hazards to digging deeper, because it can become an end in itself. "As an intellectual, I know everything therefore I owe it to myself to.." : they examine this from every conceivable point of view and come up with something incredibly complex, very often losing the main thread or impact of the situation. More situations than people care to imagine are a product of very basic things. People don't like to consider themselves as simple, therefore they ascribe very complicated and complex motivations to themselves : one sees this every day in the papers. A man is arrested for burglary for instance, and a social worker or psychiatrist or some other hideous idiot comes up and says "Ah yes, this man was deprived of a banana at the age of two therefore he has turned against society; this is his way of showing something or other."

The man is a thief. He is motivated by greed and indolence because he is too lazy to work and it's cheaper to burgle somebody's house and to profit from other people's work. Socially speaking, and he would have been considered as such a hundred years ago, he is a thief and an outcast. Now that doesn't automatically mean that everybody who is a burglar or a thief comes under that category. I will admit that there are certain people who are forced by some sort of unfortunate circumstance into stealing or preying on other people; and that is not to say that if a person is caught that their circumstances should not be examined. But the apologists should not automatically seize upon anything to make a big deal out of it in order to explain away the fact that the person is irresponsible, and has no place in what used to be called an ordered and old society.

If a person is clinically and demonstrably unbalanced, and the circumstances which have lead him into this theft or whatever can be proved in the normal and simple way : it can be brought down to what I call the "village level." A hundred years ago, if anybody in a village stole something, there was no Crown Court. The person was normally taken before a couple of elders, say the headman of the village, and the people who knew him explained his background and his particular situation at that moment.

Since everybody knew about him; he couldn't then say "I am ethnically deprived" or this is "racist" or "sexist" because they would reply "This is a load of rubbish : you are so-and-so the son of so-and-so and you've always been a useless layabout" and usually he got a good thumping and would be told "Work! Support your family." If his conditions were known to everybody and he was indeed an unfortunate wretch as a result of circumstances, you would have the situation which used to apply up to ten years ago in Afghanistan : if his personal circumstances had shown that for some reason he had been obliged to steal, then a fine was imposed on the village itself for allowing a member of their community to get into a situation where he was made into a thief. This, I hold, is a balanced situation.

Why did I get into all this? Because again, it is a question of contact and knowledge. Contact means that a person's circumstances and intention, if known, can very often be explained in a very simple way. The advent of the professional social worker or psychiatrist who systematically turns up at the drop of a crowbar and swears blue that this fellow is deprived, has removed natural justice from the scene.

In a village situation where things are looked at from a basic human point of view : "Is this person a useful member of the community?" On whatever level the answer comes back "He is a good road-mender, window-cleaner, barber, lawyer," whatever, he contributes to society and in turn society finds a place for him and rewards him adequately. This is natural justice. If he steps out of the context of natural justice and becomes a parasite, a vampire, and by whatever means, be it by threats, menace, blackmail or whatever, he lives off other people; his motivation has to be examined.

If his motivation is to control, to dominate, to extract money by means of menace, threats, cajolery or promises, he is nothing more than a charlatan. You see them everywhere : all you have to do is go to a fairground and you'll find gypsies reading crystal balls, cards, your hands, with the sort of backup menace "Cross my palm with silver, duckie, or else" ... Okay, there is pay for the job : "25 p. per gaze into the crystal ball" : I suppose it's a living and there's nothing particularly disreputable about it, but when a person goes against what is a natural order, and they are no longer just occupying the niche of the known village teacup-reader-cum charlatan, they are then actually disturbing the normal balance of that village society.

The more people exploit others, the more heinous their crime. You see people depicted as vultures in cartoons. They are not vultures, because a vulture may be repellant, but again within the context of village society, the carrion crow or vulture performs a function ; it eats things which are dead, it disposes of the rubbish, it's a sort of ancestor of the garbage men. Fine, one doesn't agress against or shoot garbage men, however noişome their profession, but since one cannot by definition have vultures in Hyde Park, one has garbage men. So a person who preys on society by using authority or whatever other lever is not a vulture; in a sense he is a parasite because a parasite uses the body in which it is a part to feed, to make itself bigger and bigger and to spread out. Again, in a village context, anything parasitical is normally contained. If a village is built on the end of a hill and that hill is being eroded away, it is shored up, steps are taken. So when, as I say, there is a situation of a negative, hostile or uncomfortable nature, it's very often more useful to see how the situation has been produced.

If it has been produced by a person, a situation, a contact or an environment, what is the motivation and the basis of the thing? Ninety-five times out of a hundred the motivation will probably be a surface one : greed, laziness, indolence, domination, a fixation or a combination of all, manifesting themselves in different ways under different guises.

So you don't over-analyze, either. One says "Don't judge the contents of the bottle by the label." All right. Well you don't ignore the label and have a swig and find it's nitric acid or something like that. If it says "nitric acid" and you say "Aha, I don't go by the label" and you take a swig, more fool you. There is a middle way between the two extremes. What is called common sense is, in this intellectual age, vastly underrated.

People say "Ha, you can't say that, I'm a B.A. Honours of Bombay" and they show you credentials of some kind. This means damn all except that you can possibly read a bus ticket. One should not subordinate one's natural inclination to say "There's something fishy about this; I don't know what it is, but I don't like it." Should one subordinate this type of feeling to say "I shall have to look at that in a Schopenhauerian context?" No. There is a long way to go toward examining a situation or a person before you have to have recourse to fantasy or intellectual labels. Human impulses are generally based on a power complex, which manifests itself in greed, domination and a whole gamut of ways : threats, menaces, "Do this or else" ... Do this or else what?

I myself will say : "I think you'd better do this." I have never ever said to anybody "Do this, or I will create hell and damnation" or "The sky will fall on you" etc. in extreme circumstances I have possibly said : "If you don't do this I will be extremely unhappy" or maybe I might manifest my unhappiness in some reasonable, predictable fashion, but this is very rare. Most of all, if I do threaten people, I threaten them with themselves : you do this, or you are being irresponsible towards yourself. You have a duty to yourself, to your family and to your society, so don't let these things down.

If you let me down, well, I want to be happy, and if I've said something which a person has ignored, I won't be; but it is neither my way, my inclination nor my authority to punish people or to call down the furies upon them. This means that my instantaneous reaction to juju, macumba, and all that garbage is categorical and has never varied, and I have no intention, no mandate, to vary it. Any menace of the "Demons of the upper air" doesn't wash : such things are a figment of a diseased imagination. In this respect, you can compare my words with any of the writings within the Tradition : nobody who had the proper authority to teach has ever threatened anybody with anything.

Why am I going on about this? Because again, it comes down to the basic intent. Anybody who threatens is using a sick, shamanistic tactic, which is all very well for the theatre or Shakespeare, but it does not have a function in real life. The intent when threatening and menacing is to make use of a technique which is basically foreign to anything in the Tradition, and that is fear, the fear of the unknown: but it is not unknown, it is known. The "demons in the upper air" or "forces of circumstance beyond one's control" which can clamp down, destroy or float about at somebody's bidding and do whatever, simply don't exist.

You have this fiendish Emperor Bokassa, who used juju and tortured people to death and ate them; but he also threatened them with every sort of horror. The fellow was paranoid and an absolute homicidal maniac, but the basic pattern to all these people is the power mania, the latent threat. This latent threat exists only if the person believes the threat is real : and what you do about it is something which is known very simply as calling a person's bluff. I give you these examples because they boil down to the intention : if the intent involved is not to benefit a person, but to extort something by force, coercion or blackmail : the weapon being used to do this is fear.

The tactics used to create or enhance such a situation are similar to the ones which have first created such a situation : if it is negative it will go on being negative, and it will produce a negative result. There is no way in which negative impulses can be fuelled by positive energy because they start at a minus. The more abysmally disgusting the tactics used are, i.e. the more negative it is, the more negative it becomes. Even supposing that a positive were fed into it, it wouldn't even bring it up to a zero level. So a nothing begets a nothing.

In short : evaluation of circumstance, or a person, or a series of circumstances can be confusing. That is not to say that you don't look at them, nor does it mean that you must inevitably not get involved with them, because that would mean completely disassociating oneself from anything, anybody, or any impacts whatsoever, which would be incorrect. What it means is : don't make too profound a judgement and don't at the same time make an entirely surface judgement. Feed in things like track record, circumstance, what one's own feeling is; don't always sell them short.

Evaluating Situations and their Abuse

It doesn't mean to say, again, that you use a totally emotional judgement in an area which requires a certain degree of emotion and a certain degree of common sense. Once again, you come back to measures and terms of reference. Don't judge overall, but don't not judge. Again, there's a delicate thing there : "Oh, I can't judge." Don't consider that one is required to "judge" because that's a big word and such a word can be frightening. If I am asked to think about a thing or evaluate it : this judgement hung round my neck for once and for all. Judgements can be modified as time passes; situations change as people get more experience. It doesn't imply, a judgement cast in concrete once and for all; these are not statutes passed by the House of Commons or House of Representatives which then become irreversible. You don't change them all the time and you don't never change them, you modify them based on experience and common sense.

After all, as English Law is constitutional law, it is based on precedent. People get up and say: "M'Lud, I quote Furness versus Furness" in such-and-such a matter, and everybody knows it or can look it up. They don't re-invent the law all the time, they update it, or update a particular element, not to fit it conveniently into a pattern, but to apply to a circumstance.

So one shouldn't feel ashamed of saying "I felt this or that" towards a given person or circumstance. One shouldn't say "Right, this is my judgement and I'm stuck with it" and hover between the two. No, one feeds the situation or the person into oneself, and based on one's feeling or one's thinking, one arrives at a reasonable feedback. Such decision as is required in the given circumstances will then be based on discussion, exchange of information, advice or whatever, and one then reacts according to circumstance. There is a flexibility : not a complete weakness and not a complete rigidity, but a flexibility.

■

Chapter 8

Tension

One thing which is fundamental to a system which is supposed to develop people, and which may appear to be a contradiction in terms but isn't, is aiming one's concentration on relaxing. This is an extremely good basis for anything which is developmental in character. When I say it may seem a contradiction in terms, it is because there is an unfortunate Western connotation to the word "concentrate" which implies an : "I am concentrating on or studying something" situation. This is a complete opposite to attention, it is tension.

Tension may be of a physical or intellectual nature, but both are inefficient and counter-productive in a useful context. Physical tension uses a certain amount of physical energy; you use a minimum amount of energy in tensing your muscles. It may be crude energy, surface energy, and one doesn't physically feel it every night or day, but the very factor of having to concentrate on something in a tense way is a waste of energy.

The same holds true on the mental level : I hate to use the word "intellectually" because the word intellectual has so many overtones, but for the sake of argument let's say that one should relax intellectually in the sense that one should not be trying to force some sort of deep rapport with something on a mental or intellectual level, because if you succeed you will bring into existence the equivalent degree of tension. If this tension exists, part of the brain is inevitably working on supporting this degree of what is alleged to be attention.

A certain part of the brain, the locomotor centre, is controlling, judging, measuring the muscles, blood flow, temperature, fluid transfer and all sorts of things. If that

77

fairly basic centre can just be running at a tick-over speed, it is helping the body and mind system to harmonize and concentrate on the issue at hand.

The basic problem with most confusion and mis-understanding is tension, both intellectual and physical. This is a sweeping statement, but it is absolutely true. It manifests itself in so many ways : in irritability, haste, sudden decisions, and all the nauseating side-effects of Western life with which one is familiar. Everybody has had things like tension headaches and a general sort of feeling of aggression or hostility. Headaches, miscalculations, misunderstandings, misheard things are often a result of tension : they tend to be explained away by various shrinks according to their school of therapy, but actually it's very basic. One feels some aggression or confusion, and it tenses you up.

There may be hangovers of racial or other overtones, but basic things in the human system are greatly over-complicated. If one starts with a fundamental basis and achieves some relaxation of certain faculties of the mind when they do not have to be engaged in a particular area, you are then liberating that area to function usefully. At that particular moment you are liberating it from any activity at all, thus allowing energy which it might unnecessarily consume to be used in a more useful way.

Therefore any of the techniques which we use can be used most efficiently when it is backed up with the maximum possible degree of de-tension. All sorts of normal or artificial aids to de-tension can and should be used; there is no shame, disgrace or whatever in using them. If it de-tensions one to lie on the floor or stand on your head, there's no problem : whatever one does, it is perfectly laudable to do it. The worst thing is to say : "I can't relax", because then you end up with a the familiar situation of a person sitting or lying in an unfamiliar and uncomfortable place and saying "I will relax if it kills me". It won't kill you, but it certainly won't relax you. The degree of effort and energy has to be correctly judged and used.

If any activity within the Tradition falls into a systematic pattern of adrenaline boosts, then you're onto a loser. It is an updated version of the memory of the first Neanderthal who went out of the cave and came face to face with a sabre tooth tiger : he needed that adrenaline with bells on. He got it and rushed straight up the cliff face or whatever to get out of the way. But a sustained adrenaline trip is not functionally useful because it needs a continual fuelling-up, and that fuelling-up is a vicious circle : the body is producing adrenaline for the boost, using the boost, and then producing more adrenaline. This is why exercises within the Tradition are based on relaxation; to capitalize to the maximum on the energy which is necessary.

Let's look at the various kinds of tension. There is muscular tension and psychological tension, what people call nervous tension : those are the two main tensions. Both of them on their own or acting together can disturb a person very greatly in his normal daily activity : eating, working, walking, doing anything, whether on the physical or psychological level. People usually know when they are physically or psychologically tense, and they don't like it. They make all sorts of different efforts and use various techniques to try and get rid of this tension, which is fine.

There are two important points which such people should notice. I have spoken before about being positive or being negative : how the negative works and how the positive works both physically and mentally. Tension is negative, and it has a definite influence, but concerning the negative and the positive, you have to learn to recognize them both, yet when you are examining yourself, something which happened, which you thought to be or which was negative, don't give that negative too much importance in yourself. It's there, it's a little bit present, it's always trying to find the opportunity to express itself.

If you go around thinking "I must not act or think in a negative way" that is all right up to a point. Beyond that point you are in fact saying that "That negative can control me if I'm not one hundred percent on the alert all the time." This is not true, it can't control you : it makes you make mistakes, it causes confusion, misunderstanding, and a million little irritants which people then put together and call "my problems." It's not that this doesn't exist, but look at it in proportion, it cannot possess you : it can disturb you, unnerve you, enervate you, all sorts of things like that, but no more than that. Once you recognize the way the negative works in you or influences your thought, you can identify it, you can say "Oh no you don't" just as you would say to a child "No you can't fool me, I know you are not a great monster with horns, you are so-and-so." Its effect on you then vanishes because it is the unknown that confuses you and causes the difficulty.

"Is this really me, or is it some deep negative Freudian or Schopenhauerian force which is working away on me?" Don't give it that much importance, know that you can destroy it, therefore recognize it and attack it with a tactic. The same thing applies to tension. You see people saying "I'm not going to be tense if it kills me!" and "I'm not worried, I'm just thinking!" Not true, this is psychological chewing gum. If you are really thinking about something, the fourth time it comes round is enough.

You don't worry your way through something, you think your way through it. There's a difference between thinking and worrying : the "Oh what shall I do, what shall I do" feeling. If you haven't thought what to do after the fifth time of asking yourself, then you're not using the right technique. It becomes a habit. "Don't talk to so-and-so now, he's thinking." He's not. He's sitting there saying to himself "God Almighty, I don't know what to do, I've thought of everything..." No, you haven't thought of everything, get back out of the problem, then look at it. If there is a solution : do it. If there isn't, wait for it. Get rid of it, relax. Do an exercise or something else to get rid of it, but don't give that tension unnecessary importance.

People say "I'm tense, I can't think." Well, that is true, tension is like fear, it blocks all the channels of thought. Somebody sees a snake : "Aaah!" That is the immediate reaction, it's perfectly normal to react like that, but if you stay like that for half an hour, something is wrong. Not only are you wasting half an hour, but it gives that snake time to get to you and bite you, which is not the object of the exercise. Okay, your reaction is such-and-such, and then that reaction produces an action. You climb a tree, you run away, you hit the snake, you scream, you do something, but you don't leave it and say "Ah, now I am all tense about this," because the snake doesn't care how tense you are, he just wants a good bite. The tension takes place because the very deep instinct for self-preservation is flooding all the channels of communication : some are saying "run", some are saying "scream", some are saying "close your eyes, it'll go away." All these things are happening, and therefore the action process stops. "I am too nervous to do something" : this is inefficient, it comes from tension.

Tension works psychologically exactly the way it works physically. If your hand is tense, the whole system i.e. the muscles, the sinews, the blood flow, is working inefficiently because one can't perform a function with a tensed-up hand. If I'm picking up an object, the sinews, nerves and muscles are working because they have measured the amount of weight they need, and are using the right amount. They're not doing that unless it's necessary to lift the object, and then they send a "we want help" message to get backup from the rest of the system. So if the communication is inefficient, the the overall system is not working efficiently. If you don't notice that your hand is tense, after five or ten minutes the body will signal it to you, you get cramp and you feel the ache; it's a signal that something isn't right.

Psychologically, if you have the same tension situation, the mental system will also signal tension, for instance by a simple symptom like a headache . It can signal to you by producing thoughts, ideas, reactions, which are ridiculous. When it does that it's not because you're going mad, it is a sign that the thinking involved isn't correct, so you clear your head by thinking "That's ridiculous". It is an equivalent of lifting your hand and getting rid of the cramp, restoring the circulation and muscular movement.

When the negative or the positive are in operation, they work in different ways : tension shows itself by anger, bad temper or lack of concentration. You might say "But why?

If I am concentrating on something naturally, there must be some tension." This is wrong : concentration is relaxed, tension is trying to force something out when it is not the proper time or when you haven't put in enough information.

Real concentration is not tension. Tension is a negative form of concentration : it shows itself by anger, nervousness, aggression, even by lack of self-confidence. A person knows they can do something : it may be a little bit difficult, it may need care, but if they don't get themselves into a clear way of thinking, they go into autopilot : their thinking becomes automatic and they just repeat a series of things they did before and which resulted in a successful conclusion the last time.

The aspect of tension is allowed in : "Can I do it? Was I just lucky last time?" Again, the negative : "Maybe it was just luck." But if you say "No, because last time I did this, and it was successful" you come to a point where some people say, "No, I shouldn't say that because this is self-pride, self-esteem, and there's an important distinction to be made here. From doing something and doing it well, you get quiet satisfaction. If you go out and stop everybody in the street to tell them how well you did it : then this is orgeuil, plus a little bit of strangeness in terms of behaviour. They'll probably be very polite, but the men in white coats will come and take you off later.

So what you are doing when you are telling yourself that "I have achieved something, I have done something" is not boasting to yourself that you have done it, because if you are honest with yourself and you remember the situation, you know how you did it, and how difficult or how easy it was, you know that you have the capacity to do it, and you then say: "I can do it again". There is no reason at all why you can't do this, and it is why we consider it very important in the Tradition that every time a person succeeds in doing something, overcoming a problem, understanding something, getting some sort of feeling, visiting a place, reading a thing, listening to some music, doing an exercise, doing a positive activity and getting something out of it : he or she should say: "I did it."

Tension

If somebody says "Ah, yes, but if it hadn't been for the training and the books you received, you couldn't have done it" : yes, but what are the books and training for? They're not to be kept tied up and hung, so that people say "Look at the books, there's so much knowledge there, how marvellous!" People like Jami, Hafiz, Suhrawardi, Rumi, who wrote them had experienced all the things that everyone experienced. They wrote things within the context of the Tradition because they knew that as long as there were people, the Tradition would be carried on, that people would need those books, that those books would be more than "Read from page 1 to the end and you're a complete Sufi" : they would start people thinking and acting for themselves. With the existence of contacts and influence and energy of the Tradition coming from different places, it would move people a lot.

The whole function of the Tradition is this. We actually don't want more people. Every time somebody says to me: "Ten years ago you said something to me and yesterday I saw how it worked," that is my Thanksgiving or Walpurgisnacht or whatever : because you can see it happening. So you say : "I did it, I put the pieces together, I worked on it". "No" they may say "Here is a book, read it and carry it about, and you'll get free passes on the buses" or something like that. No way. It's hard, you work at it; there is confusion because of your conditioning; there are things in it which don't make sense at the moment : you store them and they come out when it's the right time, when there's the need, when it makes sense. There are contradictions, which you can either philosophize about or which you can leave in one corner until you can go back to them.

Both physically and psychologically, tension acts as a negative roadblock. It stops you from acting and from thinking. It produces the inner tensions, the inner frustration, the mental blocks, because it is pumping partly correct information into a very sophisticated and complicated computer, which is the brain and the nervous system. It can be partial information on things which people like to think are right at the moment, or "I think this might probably be the right thing." Imagine you have a car outside : everyone knows that cars run on liquid. How long will it take you to experiment with every liquid in the world to find out which one you could run the car on? You can try, this is freedom and democracy : start with orange juice. But if there is a car already built, and a fuel is there and you have learnt how to drive, you do not try a new fuel every morning you start your car : it is not a new experience for you all over again. Once it is done, one does it automatically, and one then improves on it.

Once you have started the car you don't get out and say "I've started the car, I've started the car!" to the passers-by because they'll say "So what?" The car works, you can drive it, you know where the end of the road is. You do it, and having done it, you then improve on it a little further, with new experience and technique. You're driving it a little bit more efficiently. You get that quiet satisfaction that you are moving, or doing something, that things are working efficiently. If you think about it, it's a very simple answer but it's also a very complete answer.

People asked Sir Edmund Hillary who climbed Mount Everest, "Why did you climb Everest?" and he said "Because it's there." We are like explorers going to the end of the Amazon : because it's there. The fact that there exists a Tradition, a technique, a way, which is open to everybody to use on themselves, with themselves and with which to work : the very fact that it is working is proof of its existence.

The things which stop a person are the negative, the tension, the fear that grows from the negative or from the tension, the feeling of "Oh I am doing it wrong", questions like "Is it for me?" The doubts, the "God protects us" philosophical interpretation of it all are quite unnecessary. If people think that others haven't had or don't have doubts, problems, questions, times of greater or lesser enthusiasm : they all have. But this is not a measure either of their own capacity or the efficiency of the Tradition. It is a conventional measurement that is being applied here, again falling into

Tension

the same trap of : "If I study this for five years will I become king of Brazil?" The answer is no. So they say : "Thank you very much, I'll go somewhere else." Fine, let me know when you find it.

So what is all this about? What it's all about is that the negative side of the person should be looked at in proportion to the whole. It's only a small part of the person which causes the anxiety and tension, which in turn causes nervousness, doubt, and the rest of it. It all comes down to the same thing: insecurity. A person feels insecure. And the negative is there, bang, to say to them "Yes, oh it's a very insecure position you're in."

And the rather horrifying point is that because of conditioning, people will listen to that kind of thing. If you go into a room and there are twenty people there, and you say to everybody "I have a terrible problem, I am totally inefficient", they'll all say : "Yes, you are" : then you say "They all agree therefore I must be like that." You may say that they have all voted that you're inefficient, but democracy or not, they can't vote on a subject like that, it's only you who can show it or prove it. By accepting that sort of blanket judgement, you are being inefficient.

Watch the proportion of tension, watch how it builds up, watch how it shows itself, watch what it produces in every sort of disguise, in circumstances which you wouldn't expect. The negative is a very small thing, and for that very small thing, a very small victory is proportionate to its size. That is why, if it can just cause two minutes confusion, it is happy, it's done something, it's lost you two minutes. You might say "What would I do with two minutes anyway?" True. But two minutes worry is still two minutes worry, and two minutes worry at different times of the day, tot them all up, you've worried for an hour during the day. About different things, possibly, but it's still one hour's waste of energy and waste of time.

Negativity or tension which live on each other, produce each other and support each other, should be challenged, but not in any way as an equal. It's not that you don't give them a moment's thought, yes you do, because they may disturb you, so you say : "What's disturbing me? Such-and-such a thing? Well, I'll fix it and that's it." But its skill is to produce in you a confusion of attention so that you have maybe ten things to do, and you're led into thinking "Well, it would probably be better if I just did nothing ..."

You can either end up that way, or you can say : "Okay, now I've got these things to do; I simply look at them in terms of economic, social, physical or whatever priorities, and take them slowly. It's obvious I can't do all of them at once. If I do, I'll probably make a mess of half of them."

You take the things you are doing one by one, and work through them without getting nervous about them : every bit of extra attention taken from whatever you're doing is wasted time, and if you end up making a mess of it, the negative says to you "See, see? You're inefficient, you can't do it, can you?" "Well if I'd had time..." You had time, but you didn't give it enough proper attention : this is counter-productive.

■

Chapter 9

Natural and Unnatural Calamities

In an expanding universe, and in a relatively young planet like ours, there are certain natural developments that take place within the crust of the earth and within the atmosphere itself. This means that even now you get a certain amount of settling-down movements and rearrangement such as the shifting of continents, volcanos, tidal waves and things like that, which become disasters when they occur in areas of high population. When they occur in places of less population, they obviously are not disasters.

You have the purely natural shrinking or expanding of the planet, but along with that you have certain factors which can influence this type of natural disaster or calamity. There is the over-use of the limited amount of subterranean water : as industry develops it needs more and more water for its purposes, more water is used in homes as people are encouraged to wash more, cook more, use washing machines and things like that. The water supply of the planet is not inexhaustible, although it does get replaced to a certain extent by rainfall.

Rainfall itself can be influenced by the increase of heat given off by factories, cities, aeroplanes, and other things which produce heat. They in turn affect the cloud formation, the precipitation of the planet, and the stocking up of the water. When subterranean water is used in great quantities, certain strata of rock formations which are supported on these underground lakes can settle down. When this happens, you have earth movements or the shifting of continental platforms, one riding up against the other, or you have volcanic pipes which are not being cooled to quite the same degree as before, and therefore you have the magma,   the molten centre of the planet, coming up through volcanic pipes rather than meeting cold strata and forming plugs very low down and stopping the pressure; and this can very often break through the thin areas in the Earth's crust. You have industrial and domestic development which, to a certain extent, and helping these natural calamities.

A certain number of calamities could be called industrial: things like industrial accidents, nuclear piles going critical, and one has been asked if the disaster at Chernobyl in the Soviet Union was connected or not to other natural disasters.

The answer is not really : it's not of the same type. It was a disaster because of inefficiency : it wasn't a question of whether one of those reactors would blow up, it was a question of when it would happen. One doesn't have to go into the technical debate as to why they didn't take action sooner or why they didn't have a cover on it, why they allowed the meltdown to take place before they took action and that sort of thing : this is all part and parcel of the political and social conditions involved. Suffice it to say that it happened as a result of a combination of circumstances : one was the lack of technology, and there is another factor here which predisposes areas to what one might call semi-natural accidents. You heard me say before that like attracts like. At any given moment there is a great pool or cloud of negativity which is generated by negative actions, thoughts and impulses, and this negativity tends to be attracted to weak spots which exist in places of high negativity.

This means you can have a country or even a continent, which from the point of view of the human entity, in terms of the being, the human being, can be considered significantly negative. That is to say that the needs of the being of the majority of the population is not only being ignored, but any interest in their harmonious development is being deliberately suppressed. Such a situation produces greater negativity than just an ignoring, because it is a deliberate policy : it can be called an area of negativity. If you have this negative force or cloud wandering about looking for opportunities of getting together with other negative accumulations, then the predisposition for a negative occurrence is already there. Throughout history this has been noted by historians, philosophers and other people of this type, and very often it's been put down to "Divine Judgement" or concepts of that type.

Well I'm not going to say that it is or isn't true, but if one examines the evidence of history, one can see that negative situations which significantly affect the well-being of a people tend to deepen in negativity. Up to a point, things tend to get worse rather than dramatically better.

There is also an enormous amount of positivity floating around. However by definition the positivity works more slowly because it has a lot of leeway to make up. It cannot provoke something as significantly obvious as negativity, and if you judge from the point of view of negativity, the Chernobyl explosion was a tremendously obvious, evident, significant, detrimental, dangerous, negative situation. Okay, it was high-profile, but it is not at all difficult to get a meltdown like that : it is, however, very difficult to get that equivalent degree of positive energy suddenly emerging at one particular point. What this means is that it's easier to do something negative than it is to do something positive, given the possibility of taking advantage of human beings' tendency to be lazy, inefficient, sly, dishonest and whatever. Just as a pickpocket requires only a little bit of encouragement or a push to become a bank robber or a master-criminal : to restore him from his life of dishonesty as a pickpocket, and for him to become not just a respectable citizen but much more than that, takes more effort on his part as well.

It's not only the negative things which are enhanced by the negativity, positive things are also enhanced, but by definition they have a lower profile than the negative ones. You have high-profile situations which make the headlines: a passenger ship sinks, and people are drowned etc., this of course makes headlines; it's a tragedy. But if a passenger ship makes a cruise from Antigua to New York and nobody's drowned, that isn't news. If, for instance, the entire crew of that passenger ship sailing out of Antigua was all drunk and the ship was in poor condition, the possibility of a disaster is enhanced because it just needs a little bit of increase in what is called the latent negativity of the situation to take off.

That is on the scale, if you like, of the planetary situation. It also holds true for countries, groups of people, organizations and so forth. The amount of positive energy which is created and used is obviously proportionate to the amount of effort put in. It is much more difficult to create positive energy than negative, and again, how you use this positive energy is a question of intention. If one's intent is of a positive nature, the tendency will be that it will steer one towards making choices that are also of a positive nature, and which in turn will attract further positivity to the action or situation.

In the long term, i.e. in terms of generations, part of our activities can be called "energy investment". At any period of history, any number of people or a single person can, using the right tactics and given the right circumstances, put certain energies into this planet which can surface at a given moment in the future.

This is equally true for the negative. Negative situations and events have two influences : one is that they can irrigate or influence a place or community. Everybody is probably familiar with visiting a place where there may have been a tragedy or a series of tragedies, perhaps a prison or a battlefield or a place where people have suffered, and maybe one has felt uncomfortable there because it's been cold or spooky or whatever. Equally, places which have been particularly sensitized in a positive way have an influence on a person.

Negative circumstances or a negative event irradiates a place, and also project a certain amount of negative energy not so much through the crust of the planet, that's a very local influence : it puts a wave through the time-scale. You have a negative effect happening there, and depending on its degree of potential, it can surface at a future point. The amount of negative energy which is put in from an event or from a place obviously depends on the negativity of the situation, and that influences the time when it comes to the surface. Fortunately, since negative energy is less efficient because it decays faster, it cannot be projected at a precise point; it is just there in the form of what you might call crass energy, it travels through and it surfaces, and maybe it coincides with a marginally negative situation , which it can then turn it into a fully negative one.

Equally, positive energy from a place or a situation goes into the time-scale. Now positive energy can be specifically directed in order for it to surface at particular places, at very specific times. One might say "Okay, if all these degrees of positive energy are always surfacing at predetermined intervals, why is it not possible to prevent things like world wars and cataclysms in advance?

Well again, from the technical point of view, this is perfectly understandable. Supposing it is possible to predict that on October the 12th, 1989, there will be a particular civil war in such-and-such a place : okay. One can look around and probably predict the time and place and so forth : fine. Now the problem you're dealing with is not all that simple: you say "All right, we'll just shove in some energy; it'll surface in that moment, and as soon as the revolutionary leader or whoever it is steps out of his home, he will step into a manhole because the cover has been removed and that will be the end of him, no problem." If it were as simple as that, and in some situations it can be that simple, a lot of things could be done, however the imponderables are as follows :

What degree of negativity will have built up in that area between now and October 1989? Predictably x degree. If it goes to more than that, you can say "Well all right, if it goes to more, then we have underkill, and the situation won't be as bad but it will be bad." So why not overkill : double the predictable amount? Yes, but that in itself is not the only event which is happening at that moment anywhere in the Galaxy. One has to say "All right, is it possible to save say the Isle of Wight or some other place?

If that was the only patch of negativity which was likely to happen in 1989, then no problem, you can save the Isle of Wight. But the priority list does exist, priorities are always changing, and it would therefore be an almost impossible juggling trick to change them so that they would conform exactly to the amount of energy which has been put in all over, so that one didn't either overkill and have waste or else underkill and have problems.

How does that affect us? Well, as a parallel let's say it's similar to one's family or one's children : one aspires to invest in them by giving them an education, keeping them healthy and reasonably civilized, leaving them some money or investing it for them or something like that. If you say : "I will invest five thousand pounds for my child today, on the assumption that when he leaves college etc., it will be a nice little nest egg" this is based on certain assumptions which don't take into consideration the possibility of the currency collapsing and the re-establishing of barter. If that happened, it would have been better to have bought him a beetroot field, because at least he could then barter something rather than be stuck with five thousand pounds in the bank which would be worth two beetroots.

One therefore has to base certain things on intelligent or informed guesswork, and modify things as far as possible : "hedge one's bets" as they say. Now hedging one's bets or making assumptions on a global scale is rather difficult, because, to put it mildly, one can be easily over-committed, over-involved, over-enthusiastic, and this can lead to mistakes. One has to lay down certain terms of reference and priorities which one can understand well enough so that they are at least tangible. All right, they can be in the areas of dreams or visions to a certain extent, but if they are totally dream-like, then they are not tangible enough.

One says for instance "Okay, as a person, one can invest a certain amount of energy, attention, discipline and so forth, with the intention of developing oneself in a harmonious way." Every time one takes part in a group activity, it is an investment towards the harmonious and balanced development of a group, whether it be that particular group or the concept of the group. Any energy produced in a group activity can be shared with and drawn upon by another group, without detriment to the group that produced it.

Natural and Unnatural Calamaties

Any activity one might indulge in which involves the increasing of harmonious contact with other people by means of the energy of the Tradition, is automatically increasing the positive content on behalf of one's family and one's children. So every investment of a positive nature influences the future.

I said a bit earlier that throughout history things like cataclysms or plagues have sometimes been and still are attributed to "Divine Retribution" and things like that. I am not interpreting this to say yea or nay or whatever, but if you study these things, you see that there is one factor which runs through it. Some people say it's the "As ye sow, so shall ye reap" factor; there is also the "They asked for it" factor. This holds true in individuals as well as in nations, groups, parties or whatever.

I don't personally think that God has nothing better to do than create tidal waves and give an occasional swat to despots or things like that : whether He does or whether He doesn't is entirely up to Him, and I am not going to argue the matter. But the important factor here is that do such things always fall upon the so-called "innocent?" Are there always innocent victims of a cataclysm or horrendous accident? I'm not talking about original sin and that sort of thing, but you see reports that "innocent bystanders were injured" : does this mean as distinct from "guilty" bystanders? Is it the sins of the fathers : somebody once hanged a priest and therefore some generations later they become involved in some horrendous event as a result?

No, what this means is that if you look at it in a geophysical, geodetical, geopolitical way, an area can suffer over centuries or generations as a result of the buildup of the negative in that particular area. It is quite indisputable that people cannot be unconscious of what is going on in an area if it is profoundly detrimental to the people there, even if they say, "We didn't know" "We didn't care" or "We couldn't do anything about it." It may well be true that under some circumstances in the past 200, 250 years, abuses of power and things like that happened either through laziness, where they didn't do anything, or through lack of communication, where they didn't know how to get together to do something about it. All right, the judgement of time or the judgement of history has not punished a people or a continent for this.

But unfortunately for some people, if something happens in a village, a town, a city, a country, a continent, which is significantly detrimental to the well-being of a people in the cosmic sense, there is a degree of latent negativity which remains there. This latent negativity will come to the surface when the person, the people, the country or the continent are least prepared for it : this is absolutely categorical and inevitable.

It's less a "Judgement of history" or "Divine Retribution" than the fact that this negativity has invaded the soil : it has accompanied the people or whoever, and it has come to the surface at a particular time. The innocents of the second or third or fourth generation after it suffer : is this justice? Well I don't say it is, I don't say it isn't, but in fact, this is where the factor that I was talking about earlier applies. Even if you say "Okay, at such-and-such a time there is going to be a civil war" so one therefore puts in some energy here which will surface at that given time and cancel that out; one doesn't know what is going to happen throughout that period. The negativity may build up; or alternatively, the positivity may build up so that combined together with the positive energy, it will be stopped.

By the same token, you have two date points : the time when a significant negativity happens and the time when it's going to come to the surface. During that period between those two points, if a significant enough positivity occurs, that negativity coming to the surface will be stopped, and be cancelled out. This phenomenon happens consistently, otherwise you'd have constant problems, disasters and other things like that happening all over the world at almost every moment.

The important thing is that individuals, people, groups and countries make efforts after wars, famines and disasters happen : they make a positive effort to rebuild, to re-establish themselves. That effort not only re-establishes them or rebuilds what they may have lost, but it also builds up enough positive to cancel out the negativity which is coming, and doesn't throw them into another one. If they don't make that effort, either because they don't feel it necessary to do so or because they are ignorant of the fact that any of this happened, or at least allow somebody else to do it for them, that effort won't cancel out the earlier negativity.

So there is the retribution factor. It's not a punishment on the innocent : "Why should I suffer for what my great-grandfather did?" No, the real question is : what did you do during your lifetime to cancel or balance out what your great-grandfather may have done? Again, that shouldn't create a complex in the person, as in the original sin complex or "I am guilty for the sins of generations past." If one naturally, normally and harmoniously acts in a positive way, it doesn't mean to say one is always trying to cancel out a guilt feeling for what one's great-grandfather has done : why shouldn't one be positive in all activities in any case, as a matter of course? And not just to counterbalance the negative, but as an investment on behalf of oneself for the future?

Some catastrophes, be they natural, unnatural artificial, or whatever, have been meant as lessons to people when they have either become too arrogant or too indifferent, both to their own needs and to the needs of their fellow-men. Sometimes they are shown exactly how insignificant they are, for all their intellectual or industrial or whatever clout, muscle or arrogance. It is again a question of balance.

A Nation can be economically, industrially, intellectually and otherwise, very developed and proud of it : why not? Nations by definition are not humble. They can be proud of their achievements as long as they keep their equilibrium : that equilibrium being a respect for their place in the galactic pattern. And this particular planet is of remarkable insignificance in proportion to the rest of the galaxy. This does not mean for a moment that the planet is insignificant to the point that it is disposable : if it were disposable, it would have been disposed of long ago, because who wants to carry any extra dead weight? Its potential rests with its inhabitants : and as long as they are prepared to develop and invest in the future harmony of the planet, as a planet in the system, its utility will increase.

If it is not prepared to do so, and if it shows significant evidence of not being willing to use what it has and is not prepared make such an investment, it can theoretically be rejected, just as a non-performing member of any group, team or activity can be shelved. This is a cosmic justice. If people are prepared to take a proper lesson from these calamities, natural disasters and other things without feeling that they're under the Sword of Damocles, then they can learn from them.

If a window falls off its hinges in a house, the owner or the builder doesn't look at that and put it down to "Divine Retribution" : in fact, it's rust, or the screws have fallen out, which means that whatever happened is a correct and a technical phenomenon. Equally, if one looks at a country, a society, a people, a continent, that has gone haywire, there is usually a proper reason for it. If there was a system of straight Divine Retribution, why should it be long drawn out? Why bother with seven plagues, why not just have one solid good one to wipe out the lot? : unless it is that in various epochs there are peoples that attract , thrive with, by, and in negativity, and in so doing attract further negativity.

Occasionally, as corrections are made, their degree of negativity is held up in front of them as in a mirror, not to make them squirm or suffer, but in the hope that they can see what it is and where it comes from, and how it can be made worse and how it can be made better. The degree of what I might call supernatural phenomena, which can be put down to spookiness, is almost nil. Things are as spooky as one believes them to be, not really as they are.

The amount of importance people give to a spooky phenomenon is proportionate to the amount they believe in it, and if a particular phenomenon really does take place, such superstition obscures the correct analysis of this phenomenon. One says "Well I saw somebody floating about in the yard" or something like that, and the person's reaction to that is a personal one, based on their conditioning, attitude, whether they're drunk, sober or whatever, whether they cross themselves, run away, get drunk, bury their head in the sand or anything : but their reaction doesn't change the actual phenomena itself. If there are such phenomena, they shouldn't automatically a) put it down to something they ate, or b) put it down to the fact that they are doomed, because there are "three crows" which means something terrible in Donegal. In Europe a black cat is bad luck, in Afghanistan if it is a white cat that crosses your path you won't go out in the morning : it limits one's activities significantly if one believes in all these things.

There are phenomena which are of a teaching nature, of a learning nature, but there are never phenomena of a useful nature which are threatening. They may be unusual or startling, in fact they almost always will be, but they are never grotesque to the point of being fearful, frightening, and that sort of thing. Those ones can probably be put down to something one ate, or a fervent and vivid imagination plus something one ate. This is the usual combination of things which produce the so-called high-profile "Satanic" phenomena, etc.

Over the centuries, real phenomena and the supernatural have been so mixed together that any area of indicative phenomena is very often looked at from the wrong viewpoint. "The flight of swans over the Capitol showed the fall of the Roman Empire" : "see Gibbon page 72" : what happens if you see swans flying over the Town Hall? Well, you may say you're not going quite that far in your thinking, but it may be a watered-down form of that sort of thing : maybe it's just seven swans who happen to be flying from A to B.

After all, the so-called interpretative phenonomena can be two-edged. Nasrudin had been involved in some very crooked camel and donkey dealing. He got involved with it because he'd guaranteed somebody else, and this fellow had defaulted on the loan, so he was being hunted by some very savage people who wanted not only the money, which he didn't have, but his hide in any case. He was in a foreign country and he didn't really know the terrain and he wanted somewhere to hide. He remembered that he'd heard that it was possible to divine things from the shoulder blades of sheep. Fortunately, there was a skeleton of a sheep lying there, so he took off it's shoulder blade and looked at it, and there he saw a little route leading through the mountain into a cave with a tree in front, and so he thought "Marvellous!" He rushed off and climbed the mountain and found the cave with the tree in front of it and hid behind it. Unfortunately, the people who were following him came up, saw the skeleton, picked up the shoulder blade, saw the same thing, and followed him up there and beat the hell out of him.

So some things can be useful, some things don't necessarily have to be useful : it doesn't mean to say that they shouldn't be ignored. Certainly on a world scale, on a galactic scale, there are from time to time certain intimations, but it also does not mean that there are tidal waves every time Saturn is in Pisces, or whatever things these people think out. Things are there to be learned from.

It's like people who have to rely very much on their environment, like farmers, gamekeepers, etc. : they go out early in the morning and they look at the trees or the birds or whatever; they have to predict ahead from natural phenomena. Those phenonomena don't have an incredibly high profile, it will be "the moles are digging deeper this year, the hedgehogs have gone to sleep, the such-and-such are doing that" : to them, they are significant signs, they are phenomena. To the average fellow this is "What do you mean, mole?" : they don't know. They don't need to know because they tune in to the weather on the news, their life is not on the line. The livelihood of a farmer is on the line, and the information necessary for him is there.

If man gets out of his element and relies more and more on what he is fed rather than on what he feels or thinks or develops within himself, he is progressively stepping further and further away from reality. Okay, one has to make certain modifications. One may not like particular things or people or a particular job or something like that, but one can't go up to one's boss and say "As far as I'm concerned, you don't exist, you're not real" and he says "Well I'm real enough to sign your dismissal notice." Fine, big deal, you've proved that you can say it, but in a very tangible sense, he is real. Realism or cosmic harmony runs in tandem with ordinary life.

There are no great areas of compromise involved in this in the sense of "I refuse to compromise on this issue" : a person may not privately compromise with lots of things. One takes on what is called natural color or natural harmony with the circumstance. If one has the inclination and can afford to build oneself an ivory tower and just have contact with people and things that one likes, fine : but that, again, is where the imbalance exists.

So there you have a semi-answer to the question about whether these recent major accidents, phenonomena and so forth are related. In the sense that like attracts like, negative buildup will inevitably precipitate and predispose people, places, areas, to certain situations. They may not necessarily be of such high profile that they make the world press. They may take the form of localized drought or famine, but they are nearly always the result of not having invested enough positive energy as is required by the system itself : the galactic system.

You cannot be out of step : you can't be a freeloader ad infinitum where the opportunity exists to be otherwise. Where it doesn't exist, then other people can invest on one's behalf, but one has to merit that aid.

■

Chapter 10

Politics and Fundamentalism

There are several questions which constantly recur, so I'd like to mention some of them, because they are valuable issues and need constant repeating to oneself, not only as a reminder but also so as not to be caught unawares if such a situation comes up and you don't have terms of reference. Although these matters are really quite simple, they do occur with considerable regularity, and they can become problems and areas of doubt unless they're handled correctly. They involve questions of politics : all over the world these days, politics are a big business and are being pushed down everybody's throat. Everybody is being sold on politics, told they should be politically aware, politically minded, use their vote, preferably for whoever is telling them this, and everything should be politicized according to the way various people want to politicize it and so forth. In that sense, whether it's extreme left or right or any extreme, there are dangers, problems and difficulties involved, and questions constantly come up about this kind of thing.

Regarding the two extremes, a people will not have its freedom increased by being told to think and act politically. They are in fact having their freedom diminished because they are not being told : "Take a balanced view of what I say or what he, she or they say. You have the franchise, the right to vote, think things out in terms of your family, your society, what you believe in, your religion, and then vote." No, they are told "Vote my way" or "This way is the best" : from my point of view this is an imposition which in fact diminishes liberty. So what does one do? Do you then become politicized and go out and demonstrate this very minute, since politics are also a street-fighting business : is that what you do? The answer is no.

I am speaking about these things in the context of the Tradition, where allowance is made for all sorts of impacts, influences, and association with all sorts of things, including politics. You can hold very strong views, and the temptation might be great to go and shout at somebody who is putting out something which you feel is destructive or domineering or dangerous. Doing that might make you feel better, but it would be inefficient in the sense that most of these political manifestations are highly organized. You'll have your photo taken, your name taken down, and you may be singled out : in extreme cases you may get beaten up. I'm not telling everybody "Stay in your homes, the end of the World is coming" : I'm just taking things to what extremes do exist and painting a fairly black but correct picture. What then should our reaction be?

Within the context of the Tradition, we are ideally non-political. We don't support any particular political party because, by definition, our teaching is a balanced way. That doesn't necessarily mean a middle way, because that could produce something like "The middle way means undecided: I don't know whether I should do this or that." I'm not saying "Don't take any action" : on a local level, for instance, whom you vote for can be important, assuming you know the person and that he's a good fellow. It is always better to look at a person rather than the party that he represents, because then by definition he is a person whom you already know, either because his family has lived in a given place if he is local, or else because you can find out about him and his track record.

If he is preaching a cause which sounds reasonable and his track record is good, then you have a solid basis for your thinking about whether you will vote for him or not, whatever party he represents. Of course there are dangers in this, because people promise things and show a lot of nice characteristics before they get elected : after election they can become absolutely anything. So certainly vote, but be politically aware in the sense that one should reserve the right to use one's franchise and vote properly, correctly, and again, with feeling.

Politics and Fundamentalism

People say "Vote Right" or "Vote Left" but who represents that Right or that Left? Your vote or involvement should be with the person or persons, and you should use a certain amount of feeling to determine whether that person who is explaining a policy is doing it just to get votes, or whether a sincerity is coming through : your political activity boils down to a question of voting.

Now one should obviously be aware of what is going on nationally and at a local level, and one can express one's opinions. You can't go about forever saying "I have been told not to have any opinion." People do have opinions, and in the Tradition we don't suppress them, but if you have an opinion it should be usefully based as a result of reasonable thought, contact and feeling. If you say, "We are Dervishes etc., we don't have any politics," fine, but you also reserve the right, as I say, to intervene in a situation, in the context of which, whether it be commercial, economic, political, religious or whatever, one can act for the benefit of the people with whom we are involved.

So in the event of you getting into a discussion or something like a political argument : it is preferable to avoid it, because if the person is a heavy right or left wing, he will do everything he can to convince you, he has plenty of time and intention, and maybe you have neither the time nor the interest in spending that much time trying to explain yourself. After all, more often than not he doesn't hear your point of view, he just wants to convince you. If his arguments are logical and good and there's a sincerity coming over, you can listen to them, think about them and react accordingly. You don't make yourself into a vegetable : "Sorry, no opinion" : this is rubbish, you have an opinion, for instance about which is the best football team in the world, or which is the best airline and things like that. And why not?

See what sincerity and what positive things come through, see whether what you feel is correct, valuable, useful. If the fellow promises you paradise, pie in the sky, vote for tomorrow, fine : what are the solid facts in that connection? An emotional vote is one thing, you can also not vote at all, and a correct support for a political group which is in touch with the needs, requirements and capacities of the people is the vote which one should give. Is there anything we can do to counteract political conditioning, or is there any way in which this influence is harmful, say through radio, the papers, television or in education? Questions have been asked about whether one should do anything about this type of propaganda conditioning and so forth, and if one is to do something about it, what should one do, and is it dangerous for us and for our children ?

The answer is that one should not specifically do anything about it. Political propaganda can annoy you : let's say that you take exception to it, this is quite correct; but you shouldn't let it put you off balance or unnerve you, because this is one of its functions. Its basis is disinformation : the idea being to feed you enough disinformation for your thinking to become disoriented. You don't react to it any more than noticing that it is going on, and you identify it using exactly the same technique as one uses for identifying and dealing with one's own problems : you break the elements down, separate them out, and look at each one of them in turn.

Identify it : don't let it influence you, get you on the run or disturb you to the point where you go and demonstrate in the streets. There are more sophisticated ways of dealing with this kind of thing.

As far as influence on children is concerned, the influence of anything positive or negative is measured partly by their own good sense, which may not show itself or be developed yet, partly by the attitude of their parents and the contacts or conversations that one has with them. It's simply a matter of bringing them up correctly : one has and one should reserve the right to condition one's children up to a certain point. You may say "Look here, you've spent years saying "We want to break down the conditioning" : if what you say is true, you're just exchanging one conditioning for another."

Children are sensitive to mood, but they are not conditioned as yet. When people say "In the Tradition you're exchanging one lot of conditioning for another" this is not correct, because what one is doing is producing and encouraging the capacity in people to look at a thing, a subject, a place, a feeling, an energy, and then to accept it or reject it based on terms of reference which they find valid as a result of their own thinking about them, their own living with them and their own working on them. It's not "Grandad said this or that therefore we French, Spanish or English do this or think such and such a thing."

This is because one has given people the ability to produce a heightened awareness in areas where it is vital to do so : they then look at that propaganda source, and it's the Emperor's new clothes. You're not saying to them "Believe this" : you're saying to them "Look, that is that. There is the whole corpus of writings, activities and so forth of the Tradition : think of those, make yourselves part of it and look at it. If you have troubles, confusion, doubt; talk about it, ask me." So it's not a surgical replacement of one thing for another.

So you say "What about that conditioning and so forth? Isn't that a sort of undigested lump?" No it's not, because just as the human system has the physical capacity to dissolve and digest food by dispersal, oxidation, use of acids, gastric fluids and everything else; so the inner being has the same capacity, only it works much more efficiently and faster, since it is fuelled by a much more efficient and purer energy. In fact, the digestive system is like a boiler : it's a sort of crunch and acid and bubbling, but it's efficient. So is plumbing. You turn on a tap, which is a piece of technology that hasn't changed for six hundred years, and you get water from the mains; it's brought by a tube. Electricity is basically plumbing which is also brought by a sort of tube, only it's a more sophisticated tube made with wires. Then you have more sophisticated wires, and you get glass-fibres and so forth which can carry 758,000 conversations per channel and all that sort of thing.

So the more refined, exact and purer the energy and technique, the more sophisticated it appears, but actually the simpler it is. Because you're not converting up or down in energy, you're getting and assimilating the exact energy which is needed for a particular function.

When I say one should condition one's children to a

degree, what I'm saying is that one offers them the terms of reference. They are little animals : they are shrewd enough to identify and take on positive attitudes. They've got a few minor layers of conditioning, but that is no great hang-up. You're not ploughing through them, you're not breaking them off or colliding, you're providing an alternative technique. By experience, and by comparing the possibly two differing points of view of two different attitudes, you offer them an alternative to a particular attitude or conditioning which they have. They still have the old one, so occasionally they'll still bring the old one out and use it. Then they'll bring out the new one, because their minds are very active : they experiment. Then they will find out for themselves which one feels and tastes best. This is not conditioning with a capital C, of the "We're British, we think like this" type; it is conditioning in the sense that one is putting pieces of information in their way which they pick up, to use usefully.

Another topic is the recent phenomenon of what is called "the outbreak of religious fundamentalism". Everybody is busily becoming "fundamentalist" : this is an important phenomenon because it comes up again and again, and one should know where we stand in the Tradition and as individuals vis-à-vis these things.

Firstly, one should be automatically suspicious of people who use the word "fundamentalist" to describe themselves, and there is plenty of proof for this. In Iran, in Lebanon, and to a certain degree in the Sudan and in Pakistan, you have what is called "fundamentalist" Islam. Anybody can see that much of this so-called fundamentalism is an aberration, and very far from what is called "orthodox" Islam.

If a person in the United States says "I'm a fundamentalist", this conjures up the image of an honest home-grown prairie Kansas Bible-puncher who goes out and "tells it like it is" and preaches "the Law." This is fine, I'm not knocking them or saying they were stupid fools; they were for the most part good, sincere, honorable men, and they interpreted fundamentalism as being the fundamentals of the belief, which in other words, is an orthodox interpretation.

106

But when these other people come out and say "We are Orthodox; we want to establish a fundamental Islamic society" they are not orthodox from my point of view. If the word that they use, "fundamentalist" is the same as "orthodox" then somebody has got something wrong, because you will not find anybody, from the point of view of orthodoxy, as "orthodox" as I am.

In Islam, orthodoxy is considered to be represented by the Sunni, the Sunni and the Shia being the two main present-day forms of Islam. We call the Shia "unorthodox" or other things, and they call us "unorthodox" : fine, this is their privilege. In Islam, we are fortunate enough to have a book of Law and behaviour and ethics and morals and commerce and you name it, it has it, in the Koran. There is also a very considerable backup of information in the form of the Hadith. The Hadith or Traditions are the accumulation of the behaviour, sayings and traditions of the Prophet as reported by his companions and contemporaries.

The Hadith are divided broadly into two categories : the "Sahih" or correct ones, which are in the first person, in other words : "I saw the Prophet do this", "I heard the Prophet say that", "I was there when the Prophet did this" and they are vouched for by people who saw the Prophet when he was still alive. These Hadith are backed up by two, three or more witnesses : that is considered by us to be correct orthodoxy. The second category of Hadith came from unsupported testimony, but from nevertheless reliable sources, and they are called the "doif" or "weak" Hadith, that is : "My mother told me that she saw the Prophet do this ...", "My father told me that ..." or "I heard from an unimpeachable source that the Prophet did this." They are ones which are not suspicious, but they are considered "weak", and in comparison, if there is any confrontation between a "Sahih", which is first hand with witnesses, and, as it were, a second hand Hadith, then there is no question about which one takes priority, it's not a matter of interpretation. "He said he saw the Prophet do that"; "He said his mother told him that the Prophet did that" : now his mother may have been a perfectly respectable and honest woman, but a line had to be drawn somewhere, and it was drawn on that basis.

Okay. What all that means is this : you've got the textual material which is laid out plainly enough in the Koran, then you've got the backup of the recorded instances : "Muhammad said or did such and such a thing" or "Muhammad wore such and such a thing" or "his beard was like this" and so forth. Some of these things are not particularly relevant, but it is a familiar necessity to lay down for posterity aspects of the Prophet's life which people would like to know about. And why not? After all, Abu Huraira said that the Prophet used to trim his beard before Friday prayers, so I haven't got a beard, do I then grow a beard in order to be like the Prophet? No. If you have a beard you trim it for the Friday prayer because, normally and by tradition, when people go to the Friday prayer they put on clean clothes or a new suit or have it pressed or something like that; this is how they behave.

Now this is not a fundamentalist question. The orthodox or Sunni interpret the spirit of the Law broadly. You have the spirit of the Law and you have the letter of the Law. The spirit of the Law can be applied without variation, without interpolation or interpretation according to the circumstances and prevailing situation. This is essential, because as I have said before, times change, and therefore certain aspects of behaviour or techniques change too. Some things can be updated, some things don't need to be updated. The things which can or should be updated for the reasons that they can fit in and be used better, can be more efficient and so forth, always are updated : they are not modified, changed, camouflaged, concealed, or produced in a way that will make them more acceptable and praised by the intellectual élite.

To update a thing is all right : to make it more palatable by diluting it is not. This is where the fundamentalists have gone over the top, hence you get into this sort of political infighting, and I would here mention the point for those of you who have long ago lost the train of thought which I'm trying to carry out : that the Shia and Sunni schism of Islam was nothing esoteric, nothing very holy or strange. It was basically nothing more than a political power struggle. It has been magnified out of all proportion over the centuries because if you make an error at a point near the beginning, the angle of error is increasing the further it goes off over time. It was a political gambit, and you had adherence here and there and so forth.

For their own reasons and in order to explain their own points of view, the Shia do not accept large quantities of the Prophet's Traditions which are accepted by the orthodox. Bokhari's collection is famous, it's called the Sahih Bokhari, and it's made up of several volumes of the Traditions or Hadith. Bokhari was orthodox, and he wrote down only first hand versions : these versions rule out many manifestations of Shia tactics or devotional practices, and these Hadith are therefore rejected by the Shias. This is very convenient for them, but it's not the truth. The interpretation of a law or a command or a saying or a text in the form of a first-hand Hadith is not open to interpretation in a wooly way : Muhammad either did it or he didn't do it. He either said it or didn't say it : those persons saw him do it, or heard him say it, or they didn't.

You don't interpret what he meant : he didn't use seven-syllable words which were open to any sort of interpretation, because during his lifetime he himself was conscious of the fact that, as happened in Judaism and Christianity, aberrant forms of Islam could be built up based on interpretation and deliberate or accidental misinterpretation : this has taken the form of cult situations, cult figures, divinity being given out to people, pecking orders established, and all sorts of abuses.

Muhammad made things very clear : the spirit of what he said, what he did or what he taught is the one which is in fact largely carried out in Sunni or orthodox communities.

Fundamentalist beliefs, if they are sincerely and honestly orthodox, that is, based on and inspired by the original teachings, and if they are in the spirit of what that particular teaching, action, word or way of behaviour was intended to produce; then that can be considered as being in the true spirit of the teaching. Anything which claims to be fundamentalist and which is the result of an interpolative second-hand aberration is doing a disservice to itself and to Islam in general. And why I'm getting a bit anxious about this is because I find it distressing that this kind of thing should be very much on the increase, as everybody can see in the Middle East, and the same holds true for the Jewish world and the Catholic world.

The Bible or Koran or Torah-oriented fundamentalists who claim this mandate are generally pushing for power. Their mandate comes from the mob on the streets and they use it. It's a familiar thing: I saw a cartoon in The Economist the other week, and it showed a ghostly spectral figure in black threatening and casting a shadow over the world: on the back of this figure was written "Muslim fundamentalism." This distressed me, because it's not a question of semantics, Muslim or Islamic, it is that everybody is getting tarred with the same brush. If somebody goes and blows up a synagogue, a mosque or a cathedral, and the people responsible for this are so-called fundamentalists saying "back to the Bible" or "back to the Word" or "back to the Spiritual Way": they unfortunately give a bad reputation to the truly orthodox and honestly fundamentalist religious people.

In every single case of these aberrations which spring up, whether it be from Islam, Judaism or Christianity, you will see that the object is power. They want political and economic influence: it's about power, nothing more complicated than that. "You've only got a Prophet, we've got the Son of God", "you crucified Jesus, you did this": is this an honour situation and sentimental motivation, or is it, again, like poker: "You've got two pairs, I've got a Full House, ha, ha."

It is interesting to note, in passing, that the "lineal descendancy" (from that Church established by Jesus Christ) claimed by Catholics and Protestants alike, is based on much fragility.

The Church of Rome did not claim universal supremacy until Innocent I (417) and this claim is unsupported by scriptural or historical evidence.

Much of current Roman belief is of relatively recent origin; the twelve extra sections of the Creed were not promulgated until Pius IV (1564) despite the fact that the

Council of Nicaea in 325 A.D. expressly forbade any addition to the Nicene Creed. Papal "infallibility" dates from 1870.

Although the Greek Church claims "true succession," this claim is doubtful since the primitive Church, as described in the Acts and Epistles, was not hierarchical; each congregation being independent and complete in itself.

Throughout the ages, Sufis have been systematically criticized and pointed at from all sides as being anti-religious, undisciplined in religious matters, and things like that. How religious or how spiritual a person is is his or her personal responsibility, which is a grave one, because he or she is capable of developing this area and should do so : that is what we are about in the context of the Tradition.

People who preach fundamentalism do not aim to liberate, as we hope and try to do. They aim to dominate : "Do as I say otherwise you are an excommunicate" : "You can't be buried in the churchyard, you have to be buried outside on the road." How do you reconcile this with "Gentle Jesus meek and mild," love of children, and all that? Who can or did give authority to the successor to the throne of Saint Peter to deny a person the right to be buried in a sanctified place, thus punishing his family? The anguish of the family in losing this person is further increased by having to stand out in the road and hack a hole and shove the fellow in, and they and his children suffer as "Son of Excommunicate." That's a marvellous legacy of Jesus : who would get excommunicated if Jesus came along now would be interesting to see.

These fundamentalist contexts that involve the arrogation to themselves of an authority figure have basically one single objective, and that is power mania.

What I'm saying is that when one says "It's those Muslim fundamentalists ..." actually, if you claim that this is fundamental and that a person doing such things is a fundamentalist Muslim, according to the definition of what is a Muslim, by his very acts he has ceased to be a Muslim.

A Muslim is not defined by specific aspects of ritual : the ritual is representative of something. What I mean is that prayer takes on a million different guises depending on the situation, the moment, the aspect, and particularly the intention. By wholesale slaughter, killing, maiming, torture, draining the blood of people, which is literally what they do; the fundamentalists have by any measurement ceased to be Muslims by their actions, and it's difficult for them to prove otherwise.

Since such actions are specifically and categorically condemned; by contravening them deliberately time and again they have by definition ceased to be Muslims. You therefore can't call them "Islamic" or "Muslim fundamentalists" : they are not Muslim. They are fundamentalist/Shia/whatever, and let them have the courage of their convictions and admit it, and the world would then know where everybody stood.

Now there are people who are fundamentalist and very deeply orthodox, who don't go around chopping people to pieces, draining their blood and things like that, and they may describe themselves as fundamentalists in the best meaning of the term. Whether they be Muslim, Jewish or Catholic, I'm afraid the majority of them are after power. So what does one do? Again, the answer is slowly, softly, carefully : watch out. Don't get into great verbal battles : just keep it in mind. It shouldn't weigh you down, you shouldn't lie awake at night : you shouldn't have it as a terrible thing hanging over you. But acquire awareness of the situation, the existent menaces, problems, difficulties, how one can tackle them, what proportion of menace they represent, how dangerous they are, how soon they might happen, whether they're the future and so forth : at that point one at least has a rough idea of what one's action should be towards them.

It's not defensive in the sense that you lock yourself away and don't vote and don't talk to the Vicar when he comes round, communicating only by telephone to avoid contamination, no. In the world and not of the world. Know what your terms of reference are, know on what points you take a firm stand and don't let anybody rock you.

Why do I say that it is best not to get yourself into a situation where you can be provoked into an argument or something like that? It's simply best not to. Mind you, you can look at the situation : I don't say back down automatically.

Politics and Fundamentalism

If somebody says "I'm right I tell you," you don't have to say "Yes I agree with you absolutely." If the circumstances and the odds are right, you can possibly stamp on his foot or something like that : I'm not saying you automatically run away. Look at the odds, see what the situation is, or say quite plainly "I think that is a load of rubbish" or not, depending on the person.

If he's crazy enough, he probably won't notice what you're saying in any case, so he won't take any notice of you. You don't go out to convert him, it's probably a waste of time. So you don't involve yourself, you don't get in the shooting line, but nevertheless you don't compromise. It's not easy : nobody is free from the temptation of standing up and saying "Step outside and say that!" And these fundamentalists are so nutty that if you apply logic or quote Bokhari or something like that, it won't work, because they have gone over the top, they're in a world of their own.

If you take orthodoxy to be defined by the number of people promoting it, a person could get the impression that that's what orthodoxy is, and it would not be true. So watch out for what is being widely spread about as fundamentalism, of whichever religion it may be. Go back a bit, don't get scared about it : "It's going to take over!" : no. Just as one regularly checks the oil level or tyre pressure of one's car, so one also checks one's own thoughts, attitude and terms of reference, and one exchanges opinions with other people.

Don't be like me and lecture people, because a point very often comes where people listening to you just close off, and they say "There he goes again." Just know and feel the terms of reference, and use them or bring them up when the situation or the conversation demands. You don't run around scared by them, or consider that "It's the end of the world and a terrible threat to humanity" and so forth and so on. You are humanity, we all are, so let's take care of it. A person who is scared or depressed by the thought of the future is, per se, inefficient, because his or her mind is full of these extraneous things like complexes and anxieties : "What shall we do" etc.

Calm it down, think about it : what line of thought, of action should I or could I or would I take in a given circumstance, and base it on what you feel is positive and useful as far as your family, group, country and so forth is concerned.

If the situation demands that you jump in with both feet, I'm afraid that it means you've lost control of the situation. If a person loses his temper when talking about something or explaining something, they've blown it : they shouldn't get to the stage where anger takes control of them. Anger is like electricity, a good servant and a bad master. You can blow. I don't know anybody who has got as violent a temper as I have : if I want to turn it on I can go "tchoum", like that. I don't indulge it very often because it is a tool which one can use : just as one can use humour, so you can use arrogance, a bad temper, and you can also use anger. If you use it as a tool, it should by definition be able to achieve something. If you use it as a weapon, it can get out of control and control you.

So, always balanced : balanced action, balanced tactics. Balanced does not mean vegetable : "I don't have any opinion, I don't know." In the normal way of things, if you have a drink and you go into a pub and somebody says "Who do you think is going to win the football match tonight?" do you say "I don't know, either one or the other?"

Now I will tell you a joke about this very point. You know the various schools in the Tradition are in the Arabic connotation very often called "iya" which means "people of". We are called for instance in Arabian contexts "Naqshbandiya", people of Naqshband. In the Afghan and Persian and other connotations we are called "Naqshbandi" which is the same thing, the "i" means "of". In Arabic "iya" as in "Quadiriya" the people of Abd-el-Quadr.

There was a foreign ambassador who became an ambassador to Baghdad. He was insufferable, they wanted to get him out because he was such a nuisance, so they said to him "Where would you like to be Ambassador?" and he said "I don't know" because he epitomized the perfect example of indecision. The foreign minister knew perfectly well, when he asked him, that he would say "I don't know." So they said "How about Baghdad?" So he said "Well, I'm not quite sure." So they prepared everything and then sent him off to Baghdad.

And the story was that in Baghdad : this is an in-joke, so that if people think it is terribly awful of me, I do tell them occasionally : allegedly he founded a Sufi school in Baghdad. And they were called "Wiswasiya". Now Wiswas is a famous allegorical character in Afghan folklore, a sort of poor man's Nasrudin : he was called Haji Wiswas. "Wiswas" means indecisive, can't make up their mind, sometimes they want to do one thing, sometimes they want to do something diametrically opposite, and it's called "wiswas", unsure, uncertain. And he was alleged to have founded this order called the "Wiswasiya", the People of Uncertainty. And their zikr was: "Shall I do it, no I won't", "Shall I do it, no I won't."

■

Chapter 11

Focusing the Intention

I'd like to mention a few of the techniques that I have briefly spoken about before. These techniques are straightforward, and they are as simple as you allow them to be, in the sense that they require two things which are both fundamental to us in the Tradition and also fundamental to anything which is of a positive and useful nature.

First is what we call *nyat* (pronounced neeat) or intention. We hold that before one does anything, especially within the context of the Tradition, one should have a positive intention. It's no good merely saying : "I intend to this or that" or "I suppose I'd better do this and that and so forth," it has to be a deliberate affirmation to oneself that one intends to do something for a particular purpose. It's not a great consecration ceremony with bell, book and candle, it is a thing which one does to oneself with oneself as an individual, just as it is done in a group. It affirms the intention and directs the activity.

The second thing which should accompany the establishment of one's intention is the mobilization of a relaxed concentration on whatever activity or exercise one is engaged in so as to make the best possible use of the energy available. One of the particularly important exercises or secrets in the Tradition is a combination of self-examination and observation.

To digress a moment : the word secret in the Tradition means confidential. There is a difference between secret and confidential. Some people say "secrets" because they want to get a little bit of a thrill and excitement : they are doing something Secret with a capital S. We are not a secret society: we are a society of friends, a confidential association of like-minded, like-thinking and like-acting people, and what we do is not obnoxious, horrid, or anything like that. These are just our own private affairs, our own private activities. These techniques and exercises are confidential and private for another reason : if they are performed by a person who hasn't been instructed how or in what circumstances to use them, they can cause perplexity or confusion. They won't cause damage or harm because they are not dangerous, but they can cause confusion, so they are kept confidential and limited to a circle of people whose intention to use them will be beneficial to them.

Back to self-examination and observation : this function of self-examining is unfortunately common to all psychological schools and methods. It exists and has existed in various cults and things for a very long time. The point here is that within the Tradition there are very significant limits to this so-called self-examination or observation. Self-examination means that one should examine oneself, one's attitudes and one's responses to certain situations, to certain contexts, to certain people, in order to get to know oneself. For what purpose? Well, one of the many varied forms in using this is to be able to develop a predictive ability : one develops a nose, a flair, for predicting a little bit in advance what one's reaction might be to a particular thing, person, place or circumstance.

This is not the crystal ball/clairvoyant syndrome, it is a projection, saying to oneself : "Well, there is such and such a circumstance likely to come up, or about to come up or has come up, and my standard reaction, or my reaction based on my personality, past brainwashing, etc. is likely to be this, that and the other thing. There are areas of confusion, danger, hostility and so forth inherent in my reaction : therefore, knowing myself a little bit more, if it's far enough in advance, I will avoid this confrontation situation. If the confrontation is already happening I will do what is called a damage limitation.

If people allow themselves to look at and know themselves, very often they know instinctively what perhaps might happen. How many times do people say "I should have known that in a certain situation I would get up and

118

Focusing the Intention

punch somebody with a red bow-tie because I don't like red". The very fact that one knows such a thing should be filed as a piece of incidental information, but it should also be capable of being brought out in order to develop a prescience. This prescience is almost infinite, and it comes about by examining oneself.

When I say that this is both limited and yet infinite, it's not a contradiction in terms. What it means is this : that when one examines oneself at whatever stage one is, one examines oneself as impartially as possible. You're not looking for victims in the form of yourself or somebody else. You're not going to apportion blame or ascertain something awful : this is what I call the "mea culpa" or "he done it" syndrome. If you examine yourself, you apply your own knowledge of yourself; that is, what has gone into your makeup, how you may be influenced by conditioning and so forth; and you also examine yourself with points of view, tactics and strategies from within the Tradition. It is limited in the sense that you do not go examining further inside yourself than you are capable of understanding. It's no good jumping in and pulling out something which could probably very well be horrifying, terrifying or confusing, and then not knowing what to do with it. Big deal, who needs that sort of thing?

Hence, when we use the word "certain secrets" within the Tradition : if a person uses a particular tactic without knowing what they are doing, they might well reach down and take out somebody's ear or something, not be prepared for that, and get horribly distressed. Understandably. Therefore a technique is not applied unless a person has the capacity to understand what they might find out about themselves.

Stopping at this point really doesn't matter because one isn't making the sort of definitive immutable examination : it's not necessarily "This is what I am going to be, I am stuck with it, that's the way I am." There is a limit to what produces a useful feedback, a useful hind look. Part of this technique is also observation of oneself : this very simple and fundamental requirement has been pushed into a sort of cultist area which becomes quite ludicrous, because what one is doing when observing oneself really fundamentally is detaching oneself from a particular set of circumstances or a particular situation; and either before or after this good or bad situation, looking at oneself and observing how one acted. Again, not looking for a victim or looking for blame, but looking to get a lesson, to fill in the various areas of oneself by observation of oneself. It is certainly very easy to excuse oneself by saying "Oh well, I'm just like that" or "It wasn't too bad" or something like that, yet there shouldn't be a defensive attitude either, because one isn't looking for a victim.

This is very important : "That was a terrible thing I did." All right, supposing I did it. Now what do I learn from that? I learned that under certain circumstances I tend to be impetuous, short-tempered, lazy, greedy or whatever. Okay, having identified this factor that once existed in that particular situation, it doesn't mean to say that this is one of what used to be delicately phrased as one's "chief feature" : it might be a feature which has come to light under a given circumstance, but it doesn't mean that this feature is immutable. Perhaps, as one puts this plan into operation and examines oneself fairly reasonably, a pattern of reaction, of thinking will become apparent : not every day, every hour, every minute, after every situation or occasion, because this can then also develop into a preoccupation.

If, after a certain time, one finds that one has a tendency to act or react in certain ways, then one can decide that this is either a strength or a weakness within oneself : irascibility, spontaneity or whatever, but there again, these strengths or weaknesses of personality should not be accepted as being a terrible burden, in the sense that one takes the skeleton out of the cupboard, and then in great horror and amazement, one tries to force it back in again and close the door knowing it's there. No, this is ridiculous, it achieves nothing.

One gradually builds up a picture of oneself : it's not written down or built up like a prosecuting attorney would do. One examines oneself as one might examine one's best friend : one accepts a certain amount of excuses from oneself. One isn't witch-hunting : one examines oneself with a great deal of patience, but also, that patience should not exceed a certain degree. If you say "Well, I am examining myself, therefore I will be more patient with myself than with anyone else" it won't work, because that can become indulgence and an excuse; there are limits to patience as well. One has to be honest with oneself : you cannot produce a manifestly false excuse for something you have done with one part of your mind and expect the other part of your mind to accept it. It is not only a ridiculous deception but it inevitably provokes a reaction with the other part of yourself, which says "For goodness sake, I saw you making that five-dollar bill, and now you're handing it to me and expecting me to accept it!".

This is stupid. It provokes a clash and it's not a big deal, it is just a clumsy, lazy and Neanderthal attempt to fool yourself. If you fall for it, you will fall for still more later, and you will end up with dozens of phony bank notes in your account and consequent bankruptcy and all the horrors attendant thereof. You will then take them out and distribute them to other people, and that is worse still. There again, it's a whole process of situations which crop up, provoked by people's usual faults, which are laziness and, in many areas, basic stupidity.

Man is not as complicated as he likes to think he is. Very often he doesn't like to put something down to the fact that he is just lazy or greedy or stupid. Or alternatively, he can go overboard and say "Yes, I am lazy and stupid and abominable, there's nothing I can do about it and that's how I am" and "Take me or leave me." Apart from the fact that people will do just that, they have themselves to live with.

So all of this is about looking at oneself and examining oneself in a reasonable kind of way : not in an over-sympathetic manner, but using terms of reference or measures towards oneself which one has invented for oneself. With patience, with sympathy, with understanding : knowing the conditions and the situation better than anybody else; but applying certain measurements, rules and techniques, which are, if you like, standard. In most technological areas, there are standards : there's an agreed length, which is a meter, a kilo for weight, one atmosphere, one gigaherz, and so forth. These are agreed things against which everything is measured.

In the developmental area there are no such measures readily available. You can't go and buy a development meter which you clip onto your bronchial artery and it shows you whether you're developed or not, or the amount of energy you're using or not, and of course whether there is any around or not. If there were such a thing, people would spend all their time looking at it, to the detriment of everything else.

So therefore how is this measurement done? First of all, can it be done? Yes, it can. It has to be done against a scale which one learns.

■

Chapter 12

Mental Categorizations and Labels

One thing I object to in the West is the need to put a label or ticket on a person : any classification, it doesn't matter what, but if you go into a convention and you're wearing a little ticket, and it says "Two-legged baboon" : they'll look at it and say "Great!" and they'll shake your hand and they'll feel happy and go off.

Obviously in some situations or organizations, putting people in categories and giving them labels is necessary. In the army you have to have badges of rank, otherwise you don't know what the person is. In a hospital, a person has a card so that you know whether they're the doctor, nurse, anesthetist or something like that. I'm not against the categorization or naming of everything and everybody in all circumstances : it's necessary and efficient as long as it fulfills these functions. But when it gets to the point that someone sees a person in an ordinary situation, and it's a tendency, which is particularly developed among Americans : they immediately try to find out who you are, and more important, what you are. "I'm Joe" : all right, that's established, and you say "I'm Frank"; fine. "I am Utility Director of the Garbage Collection of New York City" or something like that, and you are supposed to say "I am an engineer in hydrocarbons." Fine, that's all he wants to know and he knows what the position is. If he's in the same business, he will discuss that business with you; if he is selling and you're buying, he will sell; if you're selling and he's buying, he will buy : it's all right, and there's no harm in establishing that.

Yet when you see this happening either socially or in another context, what you see is the absence of a quality or ability of judgement, or a feel, or what is called in British English "nous" : just a feeling. You look at a person, and that

Sufism for Today

so-called feeling is not going to immediately tell you that he is Chief Inspector of all the parking meters in Westminster. If it did, that would be marvellous, you'd make a fortune as a clairvoyant, but say you have a look at the person : they're reasonably dressed and civilized, so you say "All right, that person is reasonably well-dressed and well-behaved" or else he might be carrying a crocodile-skin briefcase and it's a Gucci, so therefore he must be something. Now that is, again, a ticket.

Okay, so you can go through how a person behaves or how he is dressed, but when you come to a situation where you need or must have an exchange of contact, or what I might call a "silent conversation" with that person, you don't need to know whether he is a police inspector or a jet pilot : what you are interested in is the being of that person, the quality with which they react to what you're saying, their capacity to understand, or now you should react or listen to what he is saying. People are more and more cautious about the way they talk to people about certain subjects, either because they are shy or because they don't know what common subject they can discuss with the other person. This is because very often they are not using their natural capacity to scan or measure a person : they've noticed the way they're dressed, the way they behave, the way they talk, so they have worked out their social, educational and financial position and so forth : but they don't know how to go deeper, and this worries them : they say "I don't know what to say" or "I don't know how to pitch it or establish it." It is not true that they don't know how to do this, the real reason is that they are basically not allowing themselves to : they are not allowing their "nous" or horse-sense to react.

Now this is perfectly all right in a social or party context, one has a conversation with somebody about anything : it doesn't necessarily mean that you look around the room and try and find somebody with whom you can have a deeply significant astro-physical conversation. If that's your big thing at the time, fine, but that's your problem.

The point about judgement is that one does necessarily makes various surface judgements, but one should not

124

be afraid to give oneself the opportunity and scope to develop one's own inner judgement, which one already has, but which is less and less used because there's less and less opportunity.

During the day you normally meet 20 or 30 people like bus conductors and taxi drivers and so on. I'm not saying the more meaningful and deep conversation you have with everybody you come in contact with, the bette : because this sort of person, and there are people like that, can be very annoying. What I am saying is that there are circumstances in which a person may feel a spark of contact. Now if they are wise, they won't necessarily try to put a name to it, because there again you're getting into the "label" trap : "What I felt was hatred, amusement, arrogance" etc.

It might be true that the person is showing arrogance, nervousness or negative feeling; but there again, supposing you make a judgement about that person based on a feeling : you could also be wrong. Just because I say that everybody has deep within them a way of analyzing, contacting, identifying other people doesn't mean to say that they always use all those means which they have. A simple example : you might say "I was talking to somebody the other day about nothing in particular, and they seemed very nervous." Okay, now what made you think they were nervous? Was it something deep inside which detected it, or was it that they were doing something, or behaving or talking in a way that you do when you're nervous, and you know it so you think something along the lines of : "I do that when I'm nervous, therefore that person is nervous." Well maybe that behaviour is not very tranquil, but at the same time it doesn't necessarily mean that the person is absolutely up the wall.

What I mean by this is that there are the correct feelings, the correct evaluation and assessment, and there are cases in which they are your own subjective projection : "That person behaved in a very hostile and aggressive way." Was it hostile, was it aggressive, or was it defensive? With some people, the more defensive they get, the more they are hostile and aggressive.

Sufism for Today

Obviously, as contact with people increases, one has more and more opportunities of seeing them at various times under different circumstances. When you are physically, psychologically, socially and otherwise in one circumstance, they can be in another circumstance: then it's up to you to change position. Nevertheless it's only after several meetings with a person that you can start to say : "I think I understand that person better." In using this word, most people will probably put down the word "understand" to some sort of context of knowledge : "I've identified them."

What they are really saying is : "I have got the feel of them more : their thinking, their attitude and so forth. I'm getting to know them better, and I know that if they are behaving that way, they are not necessarily just doing it right now, they just unfortunately happen to do that all the time."

This is a question of contact and using intuition to recognize someone, to go through the mask of the outside : of the Gucci shoes and Sulka tie and whatever. One has people who feel very strongly about ties, one isn't saying anything in particular about their taste in ties. Okay, Gucci shoes are probably more comfortable than Marks & Spencer ones but that isn't a categorical thing, I'm talking about contact on a deeper level, not about contact on a commercial or other level.

On the deeper human level, it is more useful to allow the contact to deepen, assuming that there is a correspondence on that level. It is a continuing and developing technique that one uses. All right, now why, or for what purpose, or how long? Do you go on and on studying a person on a deeper and deeper level? Not necessarily : it depends on the degree of contact required. It may be that one's degree of contact with a person is on a particular level, and for a considerable time it doesn't get any deeper : but on that level it is exercised, so that it becomes stronger, and it is on that basis that the contact and relationship can be built each time.

This doesn't consciously go on forever to the point where

you would say "Good heavens, you mean to say that every time I have a contact or conversation or meeting with that person, I have to start digging in like a psychiatrist to establish deeper and deeper levels?" No, once a reasonable level has been achieved, then the momentum will keep it going. But in all things of this nature in the Tradition, that is, learning something, learning to use things, learning the function of the positive : they are all techniques, and the most difficult part of them is always the first, because it involves overcoming and forgetting all the conditioning one has had for twenty years.

All sorts of conditioning is involved, and there's no point in fighting it because that provokes nervousness and tension in yourself. You don't exchange one lot of conditioning for another : that would be easy to do and it's called brainwashing. Brainwashing is exactly the same as twenty years of conditioning pushed into three months or a year : it's just pushing away at you, forcing these terms of reference, forcing these ideas, forcing these thoughts in : that is what conditioning is.

If you say, "Within the Tradition we have new thoughts, new terms of reference, new ways of generating and using energy and so forth : isn't this exchanging one conditioning for another?" The answer is no. "Is it exchanging one pattern of thought for another?" Yes, but the difference here, and this is all the difference in the world, is that it is not merely a simple exchange, because exchange is just giving one thing and taking another : the difference between learning and using the techniques of the Tradition and being conditioned is that you have the time, the technique, the contacts, the energy and the opportunity to look at these things, to read them, to think them out and do them at your own speed, to use them and to say : "Yes, this works." That is not conditioning : it is what is called using the instruments which you are given in a particular way, so that you can see how they work for you, and only then accept them.

Conditioning is the television : every ten minutes you're bombarded with "Use this for your face and use this for your feet and use that for your car" or something, and they push it in. Then you go into a shop and you say "I want something for my hair, I'll have "Slobbo" because that's the thing I saw last night on television. How much experience or conscious thought did you give to establishing that choice? If you've always used Slobbo and it works for you, then you can say "Fine, it wasn't conditioning because I've tried it and it worked and it's all right," then I would put this out of the conditioning area.

Now, to go slightly off on a tangent, there is a point here. Say one is learning terms of reference, different ideas, different ways of using and attracting energy, of examining oneself : is one just making list after list of interesting, significant, useful things, i.e. random information which one might need? No. What you should be doing is learning various things from exercises, from contacts, from breathing and other things, and you should be using them. If you take 75% of the Nasrudin stories, you see that he is applying a technique in these stories; the technique which fits the circumstance in his rôle as wise man, idiot, henpecked husband or whatever.

Now there's one person who actually said this to me : I said something to the effect that these Nasrudin stories are moral, there's a teaching element in them and that they can be applied, and he said : "Well, none of these circumstances ever happened to me." The reason I spoke to him at some length about this was because if you take a story of Nasrudin, whether he is travelling from Shiraz to Teheran and he's got his donkey and such and such a thing happens to him as a result of which he says or does this or that, it is very unlikely that a great number of people will be travelling on that road at the same time with all the circumstances being similar, with donkeys etc., so that they could exactly reproduce Nasrudin's experience : but if you take the experience in the context of another place or another time; what he said or how he reacted is as applicable to the King's Road or the Boulevard Saint-Michel as it is to the road between Damascus and Teheran.

Mental Categorizations and Labels

The story is in fact the buildup in order to leave the kernel, the centre, of that story with you : reaction, interaction, how he used the situation, how he won in a situation or how he lost the situation. How do I apply that? In a very simple way, because none of the Nasrudin stories are so incredibly complex that you can't apply or understand them. They are little simple human efforts, simple human endeavors, simple human successes, simple human failings, and if you take them out of that particular context, they can apply to a lot of contexts in life.

This is just one example of how one applies things, because in the Tradition this is an ongoing functional activity. It's not about who can amass the greatest number of books, or for that matter, learn the greatest number of Nasrudin stories : unless they can use them.

Okay, you don't use them all at once : "Just a minute, here's a situation, I must see which Nasrudin story applies to it now!" Well no, that's unnecessary; it either does or it doesn't. "A Nasrudin story applies to every situation!" : not necessarily. A modification of Karpov's opening gambit, say Queen to QB3, pawn to Queen 3, is still chess.

■

Chapter 13

Feedback

We come now to a factor which can be considered a principle : to put an approximate name on it, we call it feedback. Feedback is a principle of teaching and activity in the Tradition which has to do with information, impact, impulse or energy going out, the receiving of this, and the echo of it coming back from the individuals or place or situation. I try to avoid using the word "echo" because echo is by definition a sort of hollow or attenuated version of something going out. An echo is not what we are looking for because it would only then be a repetition of something I had already said in an attenuated or diluted form.

When I am talking about feedback on any level in the Tradition, I am talking about what I receive back from individuals, groups, places or circumstances, as a result of the impacting upon these groups, places or situations; and according to what they have received, processed, used, and fed back to me. This feedback is necessary and valuable on several levels and for several distinct reasons. Firstly, the feedback from individuals or groups takes place both on a conscious and on various other subconscious or super-conscious levels.

One of the simplest feedbacks which one gets from a person or group is a feedback of reception which indicates that people are listening : that is the minimum level of acceptable feedback. This may be a surface level or a level which a person or a group will show by the very fact that they are looking at you or in some way indicating that they are listening. They don't have to be gazing fixedly at you or sitting with their eyes tightly closed in order to sop up every last drop of this incredible wisdom, it can be a relaxed form of listening.

Now we take this process one stage further, albeit a very small and conscious step, which is interest in the subject one is talking about. Again, this attention should obviously be relaxed and fairly concentrated, without any element of tension or straining to hear and understand every last word. Implicit in first getting and secondly holding attention is that the topic or subject of the discussion should have a certain amount of interest. This is obvious : if one is sitting there saying "Rhubarb, rhubarb, rhubarb" everybody will get up and troop out. It should therefore be a topic or aspect which is interesting and also relevant, not only to the degree of intelligence or awareness of the listeners but to some-. thing which strikes a chord in them at their stage of development. On whatever level it is, it should have or at least appear to have some relevance. It may not specifically relate to every member of the group, but providing it has a certain general relevance, it slots in at another level of communication.

At the same time as one is talking and trying to impart terms of reference, knowledge, techniques and information, one is again measuring what is coming back from an individual, group or situation on various levels. The mental sensors which evaluate this are measuring simultaneously on different levels, so that during an event, a circumstance, or as a result of timing or other factors, one can expand on a point, concentrate it, modify the delivery. Just as one attempts to get or to hold a person's or a group's attention, you must also sustain the degree of attention, and increase or concentrate the attention without increasing or provoking any degree of tension.

As you have all noticed and perhaps resigned yourself to, there is repetition in what I say. In the course of the same evening I may repeat myself over and over again, or repeat the same thing in different meetings. It's not, as yet, an indication of senility on my part. It happens because : I am sure there's a term in painting or something which refers to it : if you are varnishing a surface, you don't lay down seven coats at the same time. You put on one coat and it dries, and either you wait till it's completely dry to put on another, or you wait until it's at least tacky so that the second coat will adhere onto the first.

One of the reasons for my constant "harping" : I myself prefer the more polite term of variations on a theme : is that you do not deliver a "lock, stock and barrel" concept to a person or a group or a situation, i.e. "This is it : learn and understand it because you're going to need it now" because when that happens everybody is either terrified or proud of the fact that they've been given this onerous responsibility, and they then fall flat on their faces and nothing is achieved.

It's like cooking something : one occasionally tastes the concoction, and maybe one adds a little more salt or pepper according to the concentration, the evaporation, the temperature and all sorts of combinations of things. You don't say "Well, I'm putting in this much salt, and that's all there is to it!" even though you've tasted it and it's obviously lacking in or has too much salt.

You're not stuck with a thing as inflexible as that, because when one is dealing with things like energy, the amount of energy has to be harmonious with the situation and harmonious with the capacity : you give somebody too much or more than they can deal with, and they worry, they burn themselves out, they don't know what to do with it, they've got too much. Therefore it is more efficient and certainly kinder to go along with them, to gauge them, to measure, to examine their feedback.

I am trained to do that constantly and automatically and without giving the impression that I am doing so. People might say "You just told us you do it, so what do you mean you don't give the impression you do it?" What I mean is that I don't stare at everybody in turn and make an obvious mental note, because for one thing, it would engender a certain amount of : "How am I supposed to look intelligent?" This is a process that happens all the time, and it is quite normal. It doesn't mean that everybody should look on with their tongues hanging out, or the other extreme either: all this is no measure of feedback.

The levels of communication do not depend on just one level. I've said many times that one communicates on all levels of perception : touch, taste, sight and hearing are the conventional senses, plus the higher areas of perception.

Any judgement or measurement of the feedback cannot be based on how the person looks, or even how they feel, because when you are doing this, you can get a very strong signal of a negative nature. If you are stupid enough, and people very often are : say the person is feeling ill and despondent or worrying about something or in a sort of marginal negative state : they can signal this. The most usual form is by their expression, they're looking worried or downcast. Then if they're really worried or ill, they are sending out a negative signal. They're not sending out negative energy, it's just a negative signal saying "I'm not feeling well, I want to go home," that's all.

If a person is careless, he might misconstrue this signal as being some form of hostile signal coming out : "Why is he looking at me like that? What's the matter?"

The average person can and does send out certain waves, signals or emanations, and this is quite normal and natural. Many of these are of a social or human nature like fear, hate, dread, anticipation, enthusiasm, hostility etc., and these are all received by the average person, and judged. When you have two people together one can see this happen quite often; you get somebody who is not feeling very well, and maybe they have been invited to tea or supper or a party or something, and they are sitting there and feeling unwell, and despite themselves, not deliberately, they are exuding this type of negative potential or charge.

Another person might look at them and say "Oh so-and-so's looking a bit downcast, I think I'll go and have a word with them, cheer them up" and they may do this, ask them what's wrong or try to help, and project something positive. This is not then a battle between negative and positive energies, because this negative potential is not energy; it's merely a sort of aura or mist of despondency; a sort of "down" feeling.

If this other person is in a reasonable state of health and being and thinking, and is mildly concerned that this person looks unwell, in wanting to help them, he is bringing a positive energy to work in that situation and it will usually bring the other person out of it : he or she will think and be positive, and all the various senses will work on the positive level. If there is somebody who is psychically worried or preoccupied about something and they come into contact with another person who is equally preoccupied, worried or unwell : then you get a problem, because one is going to look at the other and instead of saying "So-and-so is not looking himself or herself tonight, I'll think I'll cheer them up," they will probably think "Why is she looking at me like that?" or "Why is he behaving like that?" The negative is responding to a negative.

You can see it happen very often. I saw it taken to an almost ridiculous point in a railway carriage not long ago : it was winter and everybody was snuffling and spitting. I was sitting in a corner sucking eucalyptus and menthol lozenges, and there were two women in opposite corners and they were sort of looking at each other. After about twenty minutes one got up and said to the other "Do you mind not looking at me that way?" The other one said something like "I'm not looking at you like that, I'm just feeling awful." And the other one said "Well I'm feeling worse than you are" and sat down having scored a point, whatever that means.

But there you see the making and escalation of a quarrel, a fight, a tension situation, a sharing of despondency. You have the old glib saying "A trouble shared is a trouble halved" : a trouble shared is a trouble doubled, because you've got two people worrying about it rather than one. It's true that if you've got a trouble and you share it with somebody, they can say "Don't be a bloody fool, don't be so stupid." The other person has resisted the invitation to share in your trouble : he says "Get out of it, eh? Pull your socks up" or something.

If they both sit there and moan, maybe a third person who comes along will then get bogged down as well : "They're moaning, therefore I'll listen to their moans and I'll try and do something about it" and they become preoccupied with other people's problems, their own problems also come to the surface, then you've got a good bouillabaisse situation.

135

What this has to do with feedback is that one can lose the very simple level of one's contact or knowledge of another person or group of people. For instance one occasionally sees this type of thing : let's say that under normal circumstances, if a person is ashen-faced and is being carried into the room by seven men and a boy, on a very simple level it would give one adequate reason to consider that this person is probably not well.

On the basis of that assumption, one would either give him a brandy, call the doctor, leave town if he's got something catching, or a combination of all those things. You might say "I took it all in at a glance!" The fellow is sitting there sweating from every pore, white as a sheet, one makes the instant conclusion that "I think that he is probably not feeling well." On the basis of that, one acts : as I say, either get the hell out of there, call the doctor, or sit there and theorize as to what is wrong with him and why, and is it catching and/or whatever. "At a glance" means using just one of the senses, the visual sense.

If he then opens his mouth and speaks in a thin and quavering voice, you've got confirmation that he probably isn't well because his voice seems to be dying away. So you have confirmation with two senses : you're still on a very simple Neanderthal level. Then you go over and touch him and his foot falls off or it feels crocodile-like and scaly, so you've got a third sense, the tactile. If he smells as if he's been dead a long time, then you have this combination of very simple basic things, and you make a quick decision "He's snuffed it" or is in the process of, or has been, or should, or whatever.

The point is that the so-called psychologists and psychiatrists add to these levels by using what is called their "techniques" or "observations" and then in their mind they pull out all the files on the Freudian, Jungian, Adlerian, or whatever implications : and they accord it with the fact that the man came in and sat down in a bowl of soup, therefore he has a soup fixation or something, which "according to Freud" is a result of back-to-the-womb or whatever.

Feedback

Now they may officially claim to be exercising an extra sense, but it's not a sense : it is a science or technique which they have intellectually learnt. If a man is beating himself over the head with a club, he has masochistic tendencies dixit Freud, Jung, Adler, and Krafft-Ebbing. Everybody accepts that, fair enough, but this is not a sense. If it were called the Hammeronian Syndrome, and somebody had patented it under that name, they would have quoted it chapter and verse : so it is not a sense.

In the Tradition, we aim at elevated consciousness, so that one is not only broadcasting but also receiving, assimilating, examining and putting the traces and amounts of energy which are available from people, places and situations in the right place. One then uses it, not necessarily because one is using any conventional sense of feeling or name associated with it, i.e. "I have received energy, therefore I feel energetic" : that is cause and effect, broadly meaning "I want to feel it now. I want it today. I want to see, feel or show it immediately."

One has to accept the fact that the levels of perception one is trying to push upwards are not subject to any limitation which people may physically or consciously impose upon themselves : they are inhibited by nothing except their own lack of adherence to, or relationship with them. Now that might seem a contradiction in terms, because you say "Well, if I don't accept it and I don't believe it, it won't work for me" : not necessarily. There is such a thing as helping a person, or doing something to or for a person, in spite of themselves.

If you have their concordance, enthusiasm, acceptance and discipline, it makes it easier. But you can push through, push in or scatter useful terms of reference, techniques, and even energies : not because the people are hostile, because there are other techniques you can use to get through that hostility, but because they are reluctant to wholly and totally accept a thing when, by conditioning or environment, they are told "Only if you can feel it, see it, weigh it, measure it or recognize the colour, does it exist. If not, it's an abstraction."

What we are talking about is not by any means abstract.

137

Abstract is too ethereal a concept, it is too vague : once you start accepting an abstract positivity, then you're in deep water, because what about the abstract negativity? The latently ambivalent abstract negativity : how about that? I can't even spell it, let alone understand how it applies. Something like that can only apply to you if you let it.

If you are referring to and working in an area which is serious and real, it's a service to humanity in general and to your audience in particular that you use words which have a meaning. This again has to do with the repetitious nature of some of my conversation. If I am explaining a difficult concept and I see blank ignorance dawning on people's faces, then I don't stop and go back, I prolong the thing I'm talking about and come back again at another angle. When I see a more or less general consensus of intelligence dawning, then I can go and put another couche on top of that one.

Back again to feedback : if I'm simultaneously measuring feedback from different people, different directions and different situations, I obviously have to disregard any ir-relevant feedback, of which there is plenty. By this I mean I am not monitoring how physically comfortable people are because if you've got 175 people, and you are picking up signals from each one of them on all the different levels, with fifteen of them thinking "That damned mosquito is back again" and they're scratching themselves, and somebody is thinking "I wish that fool wouldn't put his elbow in my ear" and you're getting the comfortable signal from the owner of the elbow and the negative reading from the fellow who is on the receiving end : the whole thing would be an unreadable clutter.

One is not cutting out everything below a certain level, i.e. not taking into account mosquito bites, pains, rheumatism and so forth, nor is one putting aside everything which is abstract, because the abstract is a side-channel, a spin-off. It's not above that level, because by definition, above is "superior to" and this is by no means superior to. It's a scattering of attention, an irrelevance; people go along, they think about a thing, go down a side alley, and they wander off into an abstract concept.

Now if I pick that up as well, that could be a form of jamming. It's like the static you get on a radio : if you don't cut that out, you will then pick up things like fear. How? Because somebody has been following a train of thought, and they've gone down a side-alley, and maybe that side-alley provokes in them a fear or something unknown, and they tense up because it's unknown territory and there may be wolves or something in there, and that's what you get back. You have to cut that out.

The monitoring is specific. I'm not particularly interested in any other factors going on. This is not as inhuman or anti-social as it sounds : I don't want to know whether people are seated comfortably or not, it's their problem If they're sitting on an anthill and getting bitten, they should do something about it. One takes it for granted that they are reasonably comfortable; if they can't hear, they can shout "Can't hear in the back row!" and I can speak more loudly.It is therefore not essential to monitor all and everything that's there. It makes it much easier, because you know you're monitoring certain levels of perception, certain levels of understanding, certain levels of high er consciousness. If people leave it to me to monitor that, rather than trying to broadcast it : "We are humming on all levels, I tell you" : well, don't tell me. Either let me measure it and take it for granted that I do, or forget about it.

If one knows what one is trying to project, provoke, introduce, or influence in a given circumstance then one's brief, one's terms of reference for that specific situation, person, context, time-scale, is there. It is not rigid in the sense that "Come hell or high water, one has to punch that information, energy, or knowledge across" whether the person expires while one is doing it or not. The flexibil-ity from my point of view is that one is all the time scanning and judging to what degree that energy, information, knowledge, wisdom, technique, is getting through.

Take the analogy of a honeycomb : you've got these hundreds of little cells. The analogy is a good one because even in a little honeycomb, every little cell is octagonal :

139

clever bees, you see? With that analogy, say you take a section of the honeycomb, and you want to fill that section with whatever it is. Now as one sends out the energy, information or whatever to fill these specific cells, and as they get filled in, one is monitoring what is called the retention quotient. The cells are not just filled in the sense that you're throwing a lump of honey or dough or something at it and trusting to luck for it to stick, because if you look carefully at a honeycomb, what stops the honey from leaking out? It's because the bees put a very thin membrane over the mouth of each cell until the honey inside has solidified to the point that the membrane layer of evaporates and the honey remains. It's all dependant on the viscous quality of honey, very simple.

So back to monitoring : one can see that it has been taken up and impressed. One then slackens off from those areas which have been filled, to set them, and then you go to the next and the next and the next layer. That's why I say that a modification is possible, because one isn't just hammering away at one specific area, one is filling them all, monitoring, so that the accent is on the next layer and so on : it's eminently flexible. One can fill from the bottom up or from the top down or from side to side.

Energy is of different qualities. It acts in different ways according to the type of energy. You must remember that there are a very great number of different types or qualities of energy. The initial basic thing the energy does is to act as a catalyst : a catalyst is a substance, which, mixed with two or more materials, fuses them and makes them function. The energy, acting as a catalyst, in a sense also builds a bridge between what one might call the conscious attention effort of an activity, aided, in equal parts, by a higher consciousness.

It's the analogy of a rope between the person and the water in a well. You have to have a rope, it's a fairly mundane thing made out of hemp or cotton and it's lowered down to the water with little effort because of gravity. The effort comes in when the person has to pull up the full bucket of water. They pull the full bucket of water up because they feel a need for the water, because they're thirsty : these are very simple human requirements. That simple hemp or cotton rope is the link or catalyst between their need and the answer to their need, which is the water. So this is one aspect of the energy.

The other aspect of energies is that in the higher levels of consciousness, they are like railway lines. During winter or in desert parts of the country, they regularly run trains on every railway line to clean the tracks, oil the points, scrape the ice off, and generally maintain the line. In the human being you will often find that these contacts, lines or rails between the person's conscious state and the higher levels of perception are rusty because they haven't been used. They are not destroyed and they don't have to be rebuilt; they have to be polished up and oiled : one has to keep the lines of communication open.

Take again the analogy of the railway line : say you haven't run any trains over that line for twenty years. Suddenly you get a brand new locomotive, and you connect eighteen trucks to it and you roll it through. At the first set of points it will come off, because the rails are rusty or siezed up, they haven't been oiled, there's not a proper contact between the wheels and the lines, therefore it either grinds to a halt or goes off the rails, and it's a disaster.

The energy is a sort of scouring-pad, as well : it polishes, restores, mends, and it bridges gaps. If you like, it re-vitalizes, like recharging a battery. Again, if you take a flat battery and you push twenty-five ampères into it, it won't do any good, the shock will be too great. So you start it on a small amperage and you build it up, you measure the battery, you see it's functioning, then you can increase the amperage. You measure the discharge rate etc., and you work it out.

So energy differs : there is not one energy. There are different qualities and types of energy which are used for different types of activity in different circumstances.

There is one energy, for instance, which makes the link between a person and a building. Now this does not come, if you like, within the conventional order of things. You can say "Oh yes, but I can see a building and I can appreciate it's

141

Sufism for Today

form, shape, prominence, colour, beauty, value" : all these are con-ventional measures, or else subjective ones : "I can't stand this Gothic rubbish, give me the plain and simple South Bank concrete" or vice versa. These are all conventional attitudes or conditioning towards a type of architecture, but there is a type or quality of energy which literally and not in an abstract sense at all, makes the connection between the being of the person and stone, wood or a natural material.

This is not abstract thinking, as in : "Oh I wish I was a tree, then I could become part of that house." Very right and proper in the right circumstances, to be sure, however this is hardly possible. You can think "Oh, to be a tree and shade people!" : lovely, but again, it's abstract. To answer the question "How can I relate to that tree or that building" doesn't necessarily mean you have to go and sit in the tree or twine yourself round it. These are all possibilities, but if one accepts the fact that certain buildings or places have been constructed to communicate, and one leaves aside the spooky supernatural table-turning stuff : they have in fact been specifically built for certain functions by people who knew what they were doing. They are designed to function under certain circumstances with other buildings, other places, and with the people who exist around, visit, or see them.

If one accepts the fact that, without anything eerie but absolutely positively, there can be such a communication : why should the existence of that type of energy which makes the contact not be recognized?

Okay, let's say the person repeats the old question : "How should I feel it?" The answer is : don't push it. They'll say "I thought I heard the building trying to say "Hallo Fred" but I'm not sure, it might have been thunder" : then you get into the area of imagination and the "I talked to the trees, that's why they put me away" situation.

One accepts a certain communication without reserve. Again, it's not that you go and gabble with any particular building that you like, because then they really would put you away. ∎

142

Chapter 14

Using the Senses to Maximize Awareness

I have already mentioned the various technical tools we use in the Tradition under circumstances where for either political, social, religious or other reasons, any high-profile activity has to be avoided, for example, in a communistic political system, where anything which smacks of religious belief or anything which might be threatening to that society is automatically considered dangerous and suppressed. In a circumstance like that, it should be possible to follow an activity of the Tradition without seeming to be doing anything which is different, and hence strange and threatening.

We use instruments, words, sounds, colours and other technical means not only to overcome problems which are imposed because of different political systems, but also to overcome a physical situation. For instance, supposing a person is deaf : if something useful is to be transmitted by sound, that person would theoretically lose out if they're deaf. However, there is a colour which corresponds with that sound, so therefore a communication or transmission can take place through the colour. Equally, if the person is blind, they have the sound. It's a question also of maximizing all the senses : if a person is deaf, dumb and blind, use can be made of the tactile sense, the touch, and transmission can take place through that sense.

All these senses can be communicated with sound and they all have corresponding tactics and techniques. For instance, you can have what one might call a total inundation situation in which you have sound, colour, touch, or even a microclimatic situation as exists in places like the Alhambra and the Generalife in Granada. In a situation like that, one might say, supposing you have impacts on all the senses, as

143

is the case in Granada : by shape, by form, by colour, by sound, by touch, by sight, by smell, and by taste too, because you also have a micro-climatic situation there, as well as a saturation of ionization.

In a conssciously constructed situation like that, how does one avoid having overkill , that is, too much impact-ing at the same time? The answer is that one does not try and register each of these phenomena separately. One doesn't go round, say, in the Alhambra and look at the colours to the exclusion of any of the other factors; one doesn't listen to the sound of the wind or the ever-present sound of water to the exclusion of other elements. One takes the whole package together without trying to divide it : they are all harmoniously related, they function together as a total impact. It should not be considered to be overpowering in the sense that some people go there, or to other places, and get overwhelmed by what they call "the atmosphere".

Yes, there are certain places where the atmosphere is so tangibly sensitized that it can be even disturbing to some people, but it shouldn't really be an awesome or frightening experience. It shouldn't be something which knocks a person out, or numbs the senses to the degree that they don't know what they're doing, where they're going, what they're feeling or anything like that.

Disorientation usually takes place when a person is trying to understand each thing separately, and it's too much for them, because there's too much going on. If they then try and, say, relate to one specific thing and put it together with something else, and then add another, they are actually working too hard.

For instance, in the Tradition we use a lot of sounds. Sounds are important because, let's take a word or phrase which has a meaning. If it's being recited in a language different from one's own, the meaning should be explained so that the person understands what the word is, and also understands the concept of the word. Understanding this does not mean that every time one uses the word one has to summon up the entire concept, because that could become an end in itself.

Take a word which is one of the Attributes of God that are given to people to recite, the Arabic word "Hadi." Hadi means "guide" : that is the total concept; guide as on a path, as a friend, as a light, as an aim, as a point of reference. Its whole concept then relates to the totality. If one uses the word, one is making the connection to the entire concept. If one says to oneself "All right, each time I say it I will visualize or bring out the whole concept" there is a danger that the attention will then wander off and get dispersed. A trigger word literally triggers off the contact with the specific aspect one is talking about.

If the word "Hadi" means "guide", why not use the word in English or in French or in any other language: why not say guide? The reason we use or maintain certain words or phrases in the original, whether it be in the Arabic or the Persian, is because they have a particular sound value in addition to their meaning, and to use that sound value creates a greater effect than just using it in translation.

You also have certain phrases which have a sound value and also have a further value because of the physical use that sound or phrase is put to when related to breathing : for instance, whether the sound or phrase is said on exhalation or inspiration.

For instance, when you have an affirmative or confirmational phrase : take a very common phrase which is used in its original language. What it says, what it actually means, is firstly the affirmatory, and secondly the sound value it contains. Thirdly, in this same phrase, you have what is called the cadentic value, that is, the cadence, how it runs; i.e., a rhythmic, harmonious value. For instance, the phrase "There is no God but God" doesn't translate to the same value in English as it has in the Arabic. In the Arabic it starts "la" : "la" is no. The phrase in English would there-fore have to be : "No God but God." Usually when people translate the "la illaha illa la" as "There is no God but God" this is actually watering it down from our point of view, because in the original you have the negative, "No except illa la" : this is cadentic. One, two, tree, four : it is also said on the exhalation. By using it in the original, you're

Sufism for Today

getting its physical basis, which is its meaning; and then the over-tones, which are all positive in terms of the affirmatory, in terms of the breathing, in terms of the value of the phrase.

What this means in part is that in every aspect of every activity in the Tradition, we maximize on everything. If it is possible, if a phrase, an instrument, a place, has been constructed for the use of people in the Tradition : it is also constructed so that people can see how it can be used.

Let me take the example of Granada. Now Granada was not just an arbitrary choice "We will build a place there" : it has very specific geological, geographic, geodetic and other qualities, which indicated it as a place to be built on. It was then constructed. In the course of construction, other things were built in, and the whole place was built as a functioning machine. When you have the machine functioning, then you maximize : you see in what way the influence or the effect can be increased.

One didn't necessarily have to have water running everywhere in the Alhambra or in the Generalife, one could have done without it : it was a problem bringing it in, so that is an example of maximizing on that original situation. When you've got that, you then add the flowers : particular flowers, bushes, trees, in certain forms, not only in forms that make up certain given patterns when looked at from the air, but the actual colour of the flowers as they are arranged. When a bush or a tree or a flower dies there, it is replaced by exactly the same type of flower and colour, to maintain, to keep that design going. This is a maximization of a basic element, it's not just icing on the cake in the sense that "We will pretty it up" : it is all very functional.

If you then take this into a normal activity like an exercise within the Tradition or, for that matter any activity in ordinary life : people say, in a quite well-known phrase "to take maximum advantage of a particular situation." If a person is alert and watching the development of a situation, they can take maximum advantage of it by feeling how the situation is developing, by seeing the opportunity to build up, by taking advantage of certain factors in the situation and being ready to move in particular ways.

146

Using the Senses to Maximize Awareness

In specific and technical areas like banking, you move according to the supply and demand situation and various factors of that sort. Apart from the shareholders, you are impelled by the fact that you don't make up your mind half an hour after something takes place; you either make up your mind on the spot and it works or not, or you have problems. In a technical area, as we have seen recently in Chernobyl, if somebody is controlling a nuclear reactor and thinks : "Ooh, that's gone into the red" it's already too late to start thinking about it, because you're sitting in front of a bank of switches, a console of meters, and unless you're some kind of dumb cluck, you should have the impression that all is not well.

It is perfectly possible to look at a console composed of 400 dials and lights, and just scan it. You don't look at each one individually because by the time you've reached the last one, it's already gone into the red and you're in trouble. When you are flying an aircraft, you do not look at each switch in turn and then the overhead dials, because you'll fly into a mountain : you scan it and you know. There's a part of your mind which says to you "The hands on that bank of gauges should be all over to the right" and you see one which is moving. It's no great feat to be able to look at instruments and to scan them and to understand what they mean. The skill is in oneself.

In one's own activities in the Tradition, or in life, it is up to oneself to use the scanners or the meters, the little things which tell one that things are going right or wrong, or that one should increase this or decrease that. Basically, one constantly monitors oneself and one's own activities, again, in a relaxed way.

By definition, monitoring does not and should not mean the tension factor : "I am watching the dot" : this is counter-productive. If you go onto a flight deck and you see the man in the left-hand seat sitting hunched over his instruments and shaking, let's say you would have cause for slight worry about your airplane trip. Equally, if he's lying on the floor with a happy smile on his face, you also have a problem, but those are the two extremes.

But let's say that if there is a normal degree of margin

within the activity, there is room for manoeuvre : if something is totally committed, there is inevitably less flexibility. One can't keep it in a state of weakness, because that's total flexibility, but if you have stability with flexibility, there is room for manoeuvre. To take up a position vis-à-vis a certain thing or a certain circumstance in a very rigid sense : if it is a question or a matter of principle : yes. There is rigidity in principle. But taking up, as some people do, a series of inflexible positions vis-à-vis a large number of things : such rigidity presupposes a certain amount of tension. It's not watchfulness, it is rigidity, it uses energy. In watching all these, they are over-stressed.

In a normal everyday circumstance, a person works out certain priorities for each day or each week or each year, based on the assumption that certain things might or will or do happen : and they thus retain a certain amount of flexibility. In the Tradition there is flexibility, but not to the degree where it becomes a weakness, in the sense that it is then either a choice based on conditioning or whether or not it is convenient.

One says,` "I suppose I should do this or listen to that or do this exercise or read this." Within the measurement of practicality, things should certainly be looked at : "Have I actually got time during the day or at this moment to do it?" This should be looked at in a fairly honest way, you don't really make excuses to yourself. If it is on the basis of convenience : "Oh it's not convenient because I was going to do something which is more exciting or more interesting" they are using the wrong judgement for it.

If your priority is that you're interested in some form of development and harmonizing of yourself, you should indeed make this a priority : but not to the detriment of any of the other activities one is supposed to be doing.

What does all this have to do with the senses we use in the Tradition?

It has to do with this. If one is making decisions about one's own life i.e. about one's activities, one's profession, and if one wants the whole of the being to be involved in this process, one should be conscious of the fact that there are certain technical instruments and techniques which will doubtless help one to make certain decisions, take up certain attitudes, follow a certain pattern of thought, activity and development, and which will not usually reflect on the surface behaviour.

It's a very common and human requirement. People want to measure, they want to feel better, they want to feel improved, they want to feel more incisive, they want to get up in the morning and feel full of beans all day long. This is very desirable, but how are such things measured? Again, the analogy of the little visible meter : "I feel like hell because my energy-level is down, therefore I won't do anything" : they are measuring in a subjective way.

A person uses different sensors to measure any degree of development which they make. This is and must be reflected in their everyday activity, even if they have to take an extra two or three minutes to think things out. If you say "Fine, I have certain terms of reference or points of view with which I can run through a checklist" with a certain amount of knowledge of oneself, one should make the checklist reasonably long or short. If one has a tendency to slow thinking, then make the list as short as possible, so that there's a sort of pause, and then one does something. If the tendency is a sort of long thought-process and it lasts for fifteen minutes, it is desirable to think very deeply about the Tradition, but not to the detriment of your job, because you'll lose it. You can't go to the man and say `"You fired me! What about the Tradition?" because he may be a very nice fellow, but he also has a job to do. So therefore terms of reference or checklists or points of view or action and reaction depend also on the circumstance.

People say for instance "I am impetuous" and they do things, and sometimes they get into trouble because they use impetuosity in many circumstances, saying "Oh, that's me, I'm like that." Other people will say "Well, I have to sit down and think this out." Right. Under circumstances which don't require great thought, impetuousness is perfectly good and an endearing characteristic in some people.

Equally, if applied as one of the two extremes, it is hopeless. It is a matter of using the right tools for the right circumstance : the harmonious selection of the technique to accord with the circumstance. You cannot use a technique for every given circumstance any more than you can use a hammer, screwdriver or a saw for every conceivable activity. It has been tried, people try it, people do it saying a tool is a tool is a tool : this does not apply in the delicate area of the Tradition where one is maximizing on the correct use of techniques.

Phases are accompanied by tools. So you have to learn what the various instruments which we use are, and understand how they are used, how you can maximize on them, what their limitations are : there are in fact no limitations, except the person who uses them. This is logical, if you think about it. You say for instance that those spiked shoes which people use for climbing mountains can be used for climbing Primrose Hill, Central Park or Everest : there are no limitations on the boots, but there's a very severe limitation on the person, because not everybody can climb Everest.

Some people insist on having one particular instrument and using it over and over and over again, and if it doesn't work in all circumstances they get annoyed with themselves, the technique, the instrument : and they do a general disservice all round by doing this. The selection of techniques is limitless, but there is only one technique which is the one recommended at a given time for a given circumstance, and that is the most efficient technique. There is no choice.

If you're in harmony with a situation, what you should do in that situation is actually already there staring you in the face, if you allow it to manifest itself. If you say "I reserve the right to be free" then, certainly, you can go to the opera and stand up halfway through and play your violin. This is freedom : you get thrown out, you've proved your point, but you don't have to do this, even theoretically. You can ask people "Supposing I play the violin?" and they can then answer "You'll get thrown out." You don't necessarily have to go through the experience yourself. Playing a violin in its own context is a perfectly laudable thing, but it does not correspond with your activity as a member of an audience at an opera. This is not liberty, this is stupidity.

By harmonizing yourself with a situation, an activity or a place, you get in step with it. The context carries you along with it in a harmonious way, it doesn't push you along, it doesn't force you, you don't pull it with you. You harmonize as you go along. You aim for maximizing on things as much as possible, allowing them to influence you and developing them, just as allegedly, people who crack safes sandpaper their fingertips to increase their tactile sense. Equally, the other senses can be developed by using them and by getting the feedback from them.

All these things exist within the context of the Tradition, they are there for you, the explanation of them is there, the use of them are there, the hints and tips which are in the writings of the teachers are there. You should be keenly aware of this and then look for them, and use them more importantly : "A wise man who doesn't use his knowledge is like a donkey with a load of books."

It's no good saying "I noticed that al-Ghazzali or Abu-Hanifa did this", how do I use it within the present situation or state, and take advantage of it? But there again, before you do anything like hail a taxi or something, don't run through all the great authors from Ibn el-Arabi to now to see what they would have done, because the technique is the same. They would have held up their hand when they saw a taxi, they wouldn't have re-invented the taxi in order to take it.

If you are wandering about in a strange city and you need a taxi, say in London. If you go to the kerb in London and see one coming and you wave discreetly, nobody takes any notice. Then you notice that other people are dancing out in front of taxis and whistling, and you get the message. So it's perfectly all right to emulate somebody in that kind of area, but if you're dealing with an area which is a little bit different : if you're thinking "Just because he did it I think I can do it" : well, you might think so, but then there is that pause between the thought and doing it.

151

"I think I can do it because he did it" : but how did he do it? And then if you can satisfy that gap between him doing it and you doing it, and then do it yourself, you might be successful.There is no guarantee, but at least it possibly gives you the slight moment where you think "Maybe I can't do it." That doesn't impose an imme diate limitation on your actions, but if you're in an area which is slightly obscure, then, as we say in my country, "It is sometimes valuable to see how many grey hairs the person has, compared with your own, because people do not get grey hairs sitting in the sun."

■

Chapter 15

Gratitude

I want to talk about the feeling and expression of gratitude. In a sense, gratitude is an aspect which takes place as part of a whole context, because you have a whole context of gratitude, which is a chain reaction of action, and it is a useful tool. It is something that shouldn't be connected with superstitious reverence mingled with fear or confusion. One is not feeling grateful to something, one is not using the feeling of gratitude in a positive way to ward off some sort of punishment if one doesn't feel like it, in the sense :"If I don't openly and to my own and everybody's satisfaction feel and show gratitude by different actions, maybe it won't be noticed and I won't get any credit for it." This is, of course, irrelevant, and it's also very primitive and superstitious.

As to whether the feeling, action, or expression of gratitude is noted or not noted, this is a debatable point, because if an action or feeling of gratitude is of a positive nature, then by definition all activities of a positive nature are "recorded", "noticed" or, if they produce energy, stored.

So gratitude towards persons or things or to something has taken on a considerable superstitious or supernatural element over the centuries in the context of formalized established religion, in the sense that it has become a great threat in some religions or contexts. "Unless I do a specific thing like taking two lines in the Daily Telegraph saying "Grateful thanks to Saint Whatever" it won't work. This is not to say that a person shouldn't necessarily do such a thing, or stand up in the pulpit of a church, synagogue or mosque or whatever. There is no harm at all in doing this if the intention is to announce to other people that one is grateful for a particular thing having happened, and if one is encouraging other people to have faith in Saint Jude or

Saint Benedict or some other person, then that is perfectly all right. But if one is thinking "I'll put it in so that Saint Jude or Saint Benedict will be able to read it and see that I am duly grateful", I think they are selling either Saint Jude or Saint Benedict short, because if they have invoked the aid of the person and the thing has worked, and they then think Saint Jude or whoever is involved hasn't actually noticed and that they therefore have to put something on paper. You may say that this is splitting hairs and doesn't really matter : it does matter in the sense that a person isn't being held to ransom by Saint Jude and Saint Benedict.

Saint Jude and Saint Benedict are just being used as an example here because that's the kind of thinking one is familiar with in these situations. A person isn't being held to ransom by them in the sense that "Unless you do this publicly, it won't work." Some people may feel that it is necessary to pay public homage, or that the expression should be stated; there's nothing wrong with this, it's a perfectly reasonable and normal reaction : but the tail shouldn't wag the dog. It shouldn't be that "The spell won't work unless I actually put an advert in the paper." This is incorrect, because it is not a spell.

Expressing gratitude for something or somebody or a context affirms one's recognition of the authority or energy source with which one has a relationship, and which is helping one to achieve a certain thing, assuming it is of a laudable or positive nature. To embroider on that by saying : "It is necessary for me to undergo certain physical, spiritual and other hardships in order to prove how grateful I am" : is one proving it to oneself, or is one proving it to the source of energy that one is evoking?

All this may be semanticism or hairsplitting, but it should not detract from the intention, energy and the putting together of constituents to produce a useful situation. If there is anything extra : say one feels like writing "Thanks to Saint So-and-so" on a placard and parading up and down : I'm not against that. What I am saying is that it is not necessary within the context : if one thinks and knows one feels it and one expresses it to oneself or somebody else, this is perfectly all right. But if you over-stress it, to my mind you get a slight imbalance and a situation where there is a danger that a circumstance can be diluted, so that the person is thinking "If I don't do that, this won't happen."

At that point the mechanism gets very entangled, like harnessing energy by means of wheels and pulleys : you have big wheels and then a smaller wheel and then a loop between the two, and then you can have a smaller axle leading to a series of other cogs and wheels, all of which are acting like a step-down transformer. They've taken the energy and they're translating it : for instance, the big wheel is turning once a day. If there's a smaller wheel next to it driven by a band, that will turn twice for one revolution of the large wheel, and similarly all the way through. If you introduce more and more wheels or more and more cogs, it doesn't necessarily disturb the efficiency of this cycle of activity, but each cog and each wheel that turns requires a minimum amount of energy, maybe .05 of one erg, but it's still .05, which, for the useful function of this harnessing and using of energy, doesn't produce any beneficial effect. It complicates the issue because you have x more little pulleys to grease, more belts to watch and more synchronization to maintain.

So as more and more aspects are introduced, quite apart from the extra use of the energy itself, the person's attention can be distracted. They're checking the tension of a pulley, they're watching how something is turning, and they've got a grease gun in one hand : the risk is that the proliferation of activity becomes such that it becomes an end it itself : "I'm a pulley-watcher!" "I'm a grease-gun carrier!"

A person can correctly harness two or three of those things together : they contribute their function of pressing the trigger of the grease-gun at a moment when they feel a particular wheel needs greasing or a particular tension of a belt needs checking and tightening up. They don't frenetically use the grease-gun and check the tension of all the pulleys all the time, and continually sweep the floor in order to be seen to be active.

That also doesn't mean to say that you switch down to the minimum so that one is in a crawl situation where one is moving slowly because one is afraid that if one accelerates a bit, there's a danger that one will lose focus and one cog will start spinning faster than the other and that sort of thing. If there is a balanced decision that a particular number of cogs or pulleys will be activated by useful impulse in a harmonious relationship with a situation, there should be no degree of hysteria, frustration, worry, tension and so forth.

If you don't want the water to run out of the bath, don't pull out the plug. What does that mean? Simply this : you know reasonably well that gravity is likely to make the water run out of the bath if you pull the plug. If you do pull out the plug and then to your enormous surprise and consternation the water runs out, you most certainly have a problem, because this is well within your area of experience. If a child turns on a radio and instead of getting the usual station, hears radio Zambesi and is astonished, this is quite normal, because according to the child's limited experience with radio, Mummy or Daddy switches it on and we get the local station. This is normal and containable. If you turn it on and to your huge and amazing incredulity you get a station, you haven't learned anything from the last time you operated it. And this is a reflection on techniques.

If somebody says to you: "I will have to put on thermal underwear, a double breasted pinstripe suit, hard collar, bowler hat, hold an umbrella in one hand and a pair of kid gloves in the other in order to listen to BBC 4", he is some sort of a freak. However, since the object of the exercise is to listen to the BBC or whatever, one would be correct in thinking that all of the trappings of : "I am a BBC listener, complete with double-breasted suit, kid gloves, umbrella, bowler hat and so on" are not actually necessary.

If the person has achieved the ability to get his or her radio onto BBC, this presupposes that they can do it again without any great problem once they can recall the situation in which they first did it : they had a radio, it was plugged in and had batteries, they switched it on, the cursor

Gratitude

moved along and it pointed to a given wavelength and they got the BBC. They can then listen to it and profit from it, and even have the wavelength pre-selected to their station. Or else before doing it, it is also possible to say "I must recreate the circumstances : I was wearing my thermal underwear because it was December, I had a brown hat because I had just come in from my grandfather's funeral and I was holding an umbrella in case there was a leak in the roof" : they recreate the whole situation, tune into BBC 3 and it's no longer "Top of the Pops" because that was when they were listening then, and the time element has changed.

Now it's all right that the time element has changed, so long as they recognize the fact that they are listening to a different programme. As long as they recognize that fact and harmonize the situation, fine. But if they switch it off hurriedly and say "Good Heavens! Was I wearing the same socks?" or "Is it the way I'm holding the umbrella?" or "Have I got my hat on back to front?" : they have then gone wandering off into lots of little byways, and then you get the sacred umbrella, and the sacred bowler hat, and everything gets viewed with irrelevancies. And the intention, which is to use the minimum reasonable amount of energy to listen to the radio, gets diffused and ultimately lost amidst the panoply.

Yes, the umbrella has a useful function in its context : so has a bowler hat, so has a suit, so does thermal underwear, in circumstances which require it. As I have said before, in order to do an exercise or something positive it is not necessary to festoon oneself with tasbees, kashkuls, sticks, robes and everything else, and then trip over a tasbee and break your ankle and blame it all on your seventh personality on the right or something. No, it's just a damned clumsy and idiotic thing to do, it's no more sophisticated then that. Each thing : the kashkul, the tasbee, the robe, the stick, has a distinct function in the correct context, in the correct harmonious relationship with the person and with each other.

You can add to the use of these instruments : it is

157

functionally better and more useful to have a tasbee which has a proper thread and pom-pom. This is building-up. Beyond that, you can then go out and buy a gold box with a platinum Kufic inscription, encrust it with diamonds, put your tasbee in it and go and buy a horse to carry the casket and follow behind you in case you need the tasbee, hire a man to lead the horse : then you get a stable for the horse and a place for the man etc. At that point the function of the tasbee is being eroded; not because the tasbee itself is being weakened, but you're so occupied in earning enough money to pay for the house and the man living in it, the stable, the hay and shoes for the horse, the insurance on the box etc., that your time to actually use the tasbee becomes limited. You have eroded the efficiency or utility of the tasbee by involving it in contexts in which it is not valuable in a harmonious and equilibrated sense.

The same holds true for anything else. There's a very famous instance of one of the kings of Oud in the 16th century. He wanted to become the disciple of a Sufi Sheikh, so he secretly got information from people about this Sheikh's kashkul, and he had a gold cover made with inscriptions and diamonds, took it along to the Sheikh and offered it to him and was beaten with it by the Sheikh for having insulted him, and he certainly didn't get the point, which was quite simply that a gold kashkul with diamonds and that sort of thing is a great tribute to an artist or a jeweller, but it does not improve the function of the kashkul to be covered in gold or silver : it's better that it should be used in the correct context.

So the aspect of gratitude should not be taken out of its context and become a superstitious thing along the lines of "Unless I and everybody else is convinced of the validity of the sincerity of my gratitude, it won't work" : this is not true. As I say, I have nothing against it and am the last person to say one should not say "Alhamdullilah", "Thank God" or whatever in expressing gratitude. You don't think "I do it all the time, therefore it must be right" and it is not that if the intention is unfulfilled, one says "Oh my heavens, I forgot, can I start again?" The intention is there if one is

Gratitude

conscious of one's feeling of gratitude; it is not always necessary to put it in the form of a banner or a headline.

Gratitude also takes different forms. Much to the consternation of Anna when we first married, I have a very protective attitude toward spiders. And the justification for that is that I still feel gratitude to spiders for the simple reason that I owe them a debt going back more than fourteen hundred years. The story's well known, but I'll tell it anyway : Muhammad was being chased by his enemies and he sought refuge in a cave in the mountain. The people who were chasing him were about ten minutes behind, and when he hid in a cave, a spider spun a web over the entrance and a pair of doves made a nest immediately in front of him, and when the people arrived they looked and said: "No, because this spider's web has taken days to make and this doves' nest must have taken weeks to make." So they went off.

So I feel a gratitude toward spiders, although I don't go around shaking the paw of every spider I happen to meet, nor do I welcome certain close attentions which doves occasionally bestow upon me from a great height, but I do shoo away a spider with a certain amount of attention. If I take two or three minutes to do that, and try and prevent the dog from swallowing them, which he occasionally does, in my own way this is an impulse of gratitude which could easily get me certified under certain circumstances, but at least I have my own justification for it. It's an affirmation of this gratitude. I don't have to publish it in the papers : "Bring your spiders unto me" or something like that. But every time one expresses gratitude for something of that sort, it is an affirmation of one's recognition of the fact that gratitude is a positive impulse.

You can say "Why should this happen to me?" or "I don't deserve it" and this is all right ; a certain amount of humility never did anybody any harm. But if a circumstance goes right because an intention is right, and the energy has been properly cycled into a harmoniously correct context, then it comes as a nice and possibly unusual reward for one's acceptance and use of this energy, which we call gratitude.

Again the extreme : "I will walk from here to Constantinople on my knees to show my gratitude." Maybe, but not without suffering great anguish and being in a constant situation of physical and mental tension all the way.

Such a function is not necessarily performed by the most obvious action. The investment in gratitude pays off, and in this, I can assure you, there's no question. It is as if, in a very familiar situation, you give somebody a lift from x to y and they say "Thank you very much" and you say "Don't thank me, just pass this onto somebody else."

When you see somebody in a similar situation, help them if you can. This is the way the chain of gratitude is carried on. As long as this chain is exercised and its functioning is checked, then the investment of gratitude, recognition and intention keeps the momentum going.

It's not a stop / start : "Oh it's Tuesday, I think I'll be very grateful today, then we'll see how we go" : no. It's a re-active, instinctive mechanism, triggered off by the feeling that one is in harmonious relation with energy and circumstances, and that things have gone right.

■

Chapter 16

Spirituality and Responsibility

What one might call the spiritual area is an integral and very valid part of the activities in the Tradition. There is no compartmentalization in the Tradition in the sense that you have the spiritual and non-spiritual : both are closely related and the strength of this relationship varies on different levels : it is stronger on some levels and less strong on others. It doesn't go from weak to medium to strong ; it's a constant ebb and flow throughout all aspects of the Tradition.

I have tended to dwell very much on technical aspects of the Tradition because in the beginning of an activity, it is important that people should be clear as to what techniques and instruments they should be using, so that one can take off more strongly once any area which might be confusing is eliminated. These technical aspects must and do have a relationship with the spiritual, because nothing which is used in the Tradition, whether an instrument, an exercise, a technique, a zikr, a prayer or whatever, is removed from the spiritual. Activities, endeavors and instruments are used to a greater or lesser spiritual degree according to the situation, the need, the amount of energy available, the context, and all sorts of other circumstances. There are no what one might call constants, in the sense that a particular instrument, robe, tasbee is fixed. If it is a useful thing in the Tradition, its function is always present. Its quality doesn't change, but its function can change in different situations according to the requirements of the situation and person.

A useful thing in the Tradition is never downgraded or diminished in its quality; it is always upgraded or used in a more efficient or useful sense, with greater identification, and therefore in a way it becomes more powerful the more familiar a person is with their own intention : i.e., what are they striving to do?

Most philosophies or religions do or at least attempt to explain what the intention of their particular system or religion is. Some religions or philosophies within religions are either very vague or very sweeping. They say : "The intention is to benefit the soul" : "The intention is to create love, sweetness and harmony" : "The intention is to feel and develop a spirituality." These are all very desirable aims and ideas, but is it not more useful and precise to be more exacting in one's own demand?

A common phrase used in many religious contexts is such and such a thing is "good for the soul." Perfectly admirable, why not? But should the soul be a sort of abstract thing floating around, or should it be taken under the microscope and examined to find how it relates or where it is placed?

For hundreds of years, people have run all sorts of examinations or tests about the soul. They range from killing people and taking them to pieces to see whether there is a gap in their bodies somewhere which could house the soul that's left behind, to a very unrewarding but interesting experiment carried out in Spain, where they put people who were dying on scales and weighed them down to the last hair, and then weighed them again immediately after death to see if there was any difference. This is all perfectly desirable and admirable, as far as what one might call "pure research" is concerned.

But to digress slightly : supposing they perform a postmortem on somebody and they find something missing? What does that tell them? All right, if it is obviously connected to nerves or blood vessels, they might discover something, but by definition it isn't connected to blood vessels or the nervous system, otherwise it would be eminently traceable and detectable by normal physical examination. They might conceivably find something missing : say there's a hole or a void somewhere. They then theorize as to what it was, they know the approximate size, so they go on to examine everybody else to see whether the size is the same, whether it varies, whether it grows bigger or smaller if a person is evil etc., and they produce a whole theory from this.

In terms of pure science this is probably very interesting, but it's also very time-consuming. If they weigh a person immediately before and after death and, say they find that there is a difference of .015 milligram :what of? Of soul? I maintain that this doesn't really advance their knowledge. They might theoretically get a volumetric estimation, but you still don't know how it functions, what colour it is, of what political persuasion it is, and as I say, you are no further forward than you were before.

Trying to locate the soul has been done and is still being done : there have been batteries of ultraviolet, infrared and other cameras focused on people who are expiring in order to catch this "balloon" or whatever floating upwards. I think that it won't really advance the identification or understanding of the soul in any valuable way. After great research, it could conceivably produce many academic tomes showing how the measurements were done : among whom; whether there were genetic or racial variations; what the ambient temperature was etc. But a reasonable and normally educated person has neither the time nor the inclination to read through massive volumes to try and answer a fairly simple question, that is, what is the soul?

How does one relate to the soul and these certain reasonable, fundamental things? Supposing, in the impossible situation that a soul was discovered in somebody who had died, and dissected, and the full chemical and other analysis of the soul was published : it wouldn't mean anything to the people who are interested in the spiritual character of the soul. So where does that leave us? I think it leaves us in the position where one says "On the basis of my feelings, my experience, and from sources I trust and respect, I will try and build up a vague, albeit imprecise personal idea, not so much of "the soul" as such, but if you like, of the function of the soul."

Supposing one goes back a bit to the most ancient

writings, by people who were not blessed with highly intellectual preoccupations. They weren't confused, and they didn't worry about anatomical, physiological and other aspects : they were trying to explain what man's soul was, what it's function was in relation to the person, in relation to God, in relation to the relationship one has with God and the Cosmos, and the whole picture. You have to start somewhere : so people started analyzing and trying to understand the function of the soul. Many of them got carried away and wrote enormous tomes which were probably very valuable and sincere, but they didn't actually help people to use any specific things which they discovered.

Therefore if one goes back a little bit to the ancient writers who posed questions which were very simple and which they felt deeply and sincerely, one has the basis of the idea that, for one thing, a person has a soul, fine. For the moment let's not go into other realms of deciding where it came from with the attendant debates about its size and whatever, let us accept the premise that a person has a soul as a fact. Cutting out a lot of excess comment and things like that, one finds that throughout various ages, philosophical systems and religions, a lot of the authorities agreed that there is a soul; and that the usual idea behind belief, faith, effort, and similar activities was to develop the soul in harmony with other developments.

The people involved in this were not necessarily by any means concerned with "up to what point can man develop his soul?" They accepted what we accept in the Tradition, the premise that the soul is capable of infinite development. It is important that one is not aiming to develop the soul up to x or y point or something like that, because that puts it into the realm of the conventional, and the measurement then becomes a sort of competition : "How is your soul doing? Very nicely, I'm up to such-and-such, how about yours?" and "His soul isn't very good." It becomes a competition and confusion ensues.

So to every man his soul, to every man his responsibility : and here we get a very good nudge and

164

indication into what they were thinking and talking about when they wrote about "man's responsibility to himself." They said perfectly rightly that in a person's harmonious development, one normally aspires to different degrees and areas of development and progress, be it educational, financial, social, or if they want, political or yet other developments. These are perfectly normal aspirations; they combine with reasonable ambition and enthusiasm to develop these areas, and all these aspects of effort and development are also related to man's responsibility to his own soul.

Just as by any measure, it is irresponsible for a person to deliberately damage their body by bashing themselves with something, it is also irresponsible of them to damage for no reason any educational, commercial, social, or other development which they have achieved. It is an irresponsible act to do this. Neglect is also irresponsible : allowing any development, say educational, physical, social, economic, or whatever to disappear or be damaged or degenerate because of lack of attention is irresponsible. By the same token it is also irresponsible for a person to ignore the possibility of development in relation to their soul, in relation to their spiritual development.

We now come into an area which is very much more personal, and which becomes very much more the absolute responsibility of the person. A person will say "I owe it to myself", "my family", "my standing in society" or whatever, to let's say "have a good standard of living", "bring up my children reasonably", "look after my family", "shoulder my responsibilities" and all these things.

A person does some of these things for other people, for their family for instance : either because they like their family or because they're obliged to by law, or they do things for the people next door to show off, or for their friends at college or whatever. So a certain amount of effort or so-called responsibility is taken on for other people. It is taken on for other people because a person takes it on willingly : say for children, family and friends. Some of these responsibilities are imposed because one has to maintain a certain standard of living, a certain social level: all right, this is not terrible, it's a normal situation; but the thing which is imposed by the person's own feeling of responsibility is the developing and the servicing of their own soul.

No matter how strictly they have been brought up, under whatever religious system and even if they are badgered by priests of every denomination for 24 hours a day seven days of the week to pray, fast, believe and do this and that : only they themselves know and feel whether they're going through a mumbo-jumbo ritual, or whether they're really communicating and truly feeling any sort of development. It is the most intensely personal thing. After all, they are obviously uniquely placed to communicate feelings, information and valuable things by which they develop themselves spiritually.

In the Tradition, our estimation is that the person's soul is always alert; that is to say that it doesn't necessarily mean that if the person does not make the effort, they will not absorb useful and valuable spiritual things : they will, they can't really avoid it. But it is very much more beneficial for their spiritual development to relate to something which will help them to nourish their spiritual state.

A person who is conscious of a spiritual need does not necessarily have to define what precise degree of spiritual need it is. It can be helpful; sometimes it can be a hindrance, because if they consider that their spiritual need is of a certain type and it is not readily available or if they can't find it with a little bit of effort, they may either become depressed and disturbed and feel deprived, or else they might go off to some far-flung place and find out that in reality it was not what they needed. It boils down to the old question : is a person deciding what they need or what they want? This can be two very different things.

So one looks upon the spiritual development of the soul as an extremely important part of one's responsibility, in harmony with other activities. Again, you can take this to an extreme and you can look at that spiritual development as being the most "important" activity to the exclusion of everything else.

You have perfectly good people in nunneries and monasteries where people are supposed to be constantly vigilant about their souls : I'm not for a moment saying anything against these people; they do a very great deal of good. My only feeling in relation to monks and nuns is that their total usefulness is limited by their very often self-imposed exclusion from harmonious relationship with all the other things which surround them. They do a great deal of good : but they could do actually more good if they came out of their seclusion a little bit, and lived less with the total and wholly spiritual preoccupation which prevents them from functioning at really 100%.

The amount of time which one spends in spiritual activity, thought and action is not as important as the quality of that time. If one gabbles through many prayers or tasbees or rosaries or things like that, it can become a sort of quantitative consumption, and of course the risk is that the measurement automatically gets into a mundane area. One is talking, then, about time. "I spent a half-an-hour praying" and somebody else says "I prayed for two hours" and the person who spent only half an hour feels down, so the next time they pray for two and a half hours and the other one then spends three hours at it, and so the rat race thing goes on.

I'm not saying that the duration of a prayer or spiritual activity has no relation to the time element at all ; it certainly does. I have already explained that if one is going to do a exercise , or read or do something in that area, one should set aside a certain time, a preparatory period during which one is detaching slightly from everyday things; and then go into the operational period : and then take another short period to come out and go on with one's normal activities. This is necessary and useful, because not only is one switching off slightly from the distractions of everyday life, one is telling oneself that one is doing it as well, so that it's marking the actual activity. One isn't detaching oneself entirely, and one isn't expected to go into a trance or anything like that.

The time element is not unimportant, but it is not the unique measurement, because if one has developed the capacity or technique, one can do a zikr, recitation, or put oneself in a positive frame of mind for one, two or five minutes while one is in the back of a taxi or something, switching off deliberately without having to go into a trance or miss one's station : it's just being out of the moment-um and turmoil for a reasonably short period.

So there is a responsibility on which one has to align oneself and then take advantage of the availability of advice, direction, energy in the spiritual area, and this re-sponsibility is very considerable. It should not become a preoccupation, so that a person is scurrying from church to church or mosque to mosque and spending all their time on their knees, because that can become an end in itself. You have the compulsive pilgrim who is rushing from one shrine to another : very devoted and soulful, but using up a lot of energy on things like the collection of relics, and less time on actually familiarizing themselves with them and using them.

There is a fellow I haven't seen for twenty years, but the last time I saw him, and I assure you, this is a true story, not one of your travellers' tales : he was building a sort of tiny log cabin in a little village south of Jerusalem ; he was a Copt, and he had completed three walls and part of the roof in wood; and his ambition in life was to complete the fourth wall. It was a small cabin, but he had done pretty well because he was constructing this out of the wood from the Holy Cross, and as I say, he'd done pretty well to get three walls and a roof out of just one cross. But there are three or four factories in the Holy Land which produce such frag-ments.

I'm ashamed to say that one shop directly opposite the Dome of the Rock in Jerusalem was being run years ago by an Afghan trader whose son spent most of his time chopping up orange crates in the back of the shop and staining them dark brown, and he was well known as a good source of quite large pieces of the True Cross. This is not as ridiculous as it sounds, and whether he actually completed the hut or not, I don't know, but the point is this : that there you have a very devout and knowledgeable man, but with a fixation that he had to do this : after he has completed it, the question is what is he going to do and what is it going to do for him? Is this an implicit defense against the malefic influences of the Demons of the Upper Air, or will he float away on it when another flood comes? The entire day and night energies of this man was devoted to seeking out this material, despite the fact that there was every evidence that this stuff was being chopped up from old railway sleepers and things like that.

So if a person is a compulsive pilgrim or collects holy relics and other things like that, he does it for an idolatrous idea, meaning that he constructs some sort of effigy and does something with it. If you go back as far as history has recorded and even before, the whole idea of the relic is that it has a function. It is not just a good-luck talisman, a piece of St. Cuthbert's left toenail, it is supposed to have a function : people brought saintly relics from various parts of the world, and they built cathedrals and places like that to house them. This is perfectly correct, because after all it honored the name of the holy person or saint or whatever : the function being to create a house of God, a meeting place, a sanctuary, and by implication, the relic of that person according to our estimation or measurement in the Tradition, would attract a certain amount of positive energy which would be at the disposal of the people who visited that place or participated in any activity there. So it is a functional thing.

One hears Medieval phrases like : "By doing such-and-such, or by such-and-such a voyage or pilgrimage, a person nourished their soul" and people say : "Oh how quaint." Well, if you look at it, this is literally true. "Nourish" means not only to feed : if you look in the dictionary, you will see it means to sustain, to feed, and also to benefit : there you have the whole concept. So when they say that a person is nourishing his soul, it doesn't mean to say that he was ramming a tube down his throat and pouring

Holy Water through it : there are, incidentally, for your elucidation, medieval manuscripts showing just that : holy men with medieval funnels thrust down their throats, and getting, I don't know, inhibited I would think, but that's their own concern.

Work it out on that basis : this contact, use of energy, spiritual activity, does literally nourish the soul. On that assumption, if you do nourish something, it usually by definition grows in size, in stature, in authority, in value. Nourishing something cannot be counter- productive. Of course you can say "Well I feed a wolf and it'll go out and eat people. "Well yes, if you want to split hairs, the person who is feeding a wolf and letting it loose is not nourishing, he is just feeding wolves at other people's expense.

If you are nourishing something, by definition you are not only caring for and showing that you have some identification with it, because otherwise you would not bother; you are helping it to grow, develop, increase in stature, increase in value, increase in influence. Increase in influence over what? Over yourself, not over other people. Because by definition within the Tradition, the development of a person's soul enables him or her to establish a certain form of ascendancy over other people in a teaching or beneficial area. Other things which go with it are not incidental, but they are a result of that form of development.

That is not to say automatically that the more one de- velops the soul, the bigger one's bank balance : very few of the people we would consider to be developed have died as millionaires. But the spin-off or influence of a spiritually developed person cannot be denied; by definition their influence is and has to be of a beneficial nature. If you have a so-called spiritual leader and he is bananas, if what he does is deleterious to or suppresses the development of the liberty of a great number of people, then by definition, he is not a spiritual leader.

If you have a leader who does not claim to be spiritual, who claims to be a president or a ruler by statute or fiat or whatever, then fine, he can do good, bad, or anything in between. But the claim to elevated spirituality must be

Spirituality and Responsibility

accompanied by a commensurate benevolent influence, otherwise it does not reflect any degree of useful, viable, and positive spirituality.

For the moment, let us define in a fairly reasonable and relaxed way what one considers one's duty to one's soul to be, and in what way one can discharge this responsibility within the context of one's harmonious existence in the world and towards other people. The priorities do not clash in the sense that : "Oh, I can't do a day's work because I should be going to x sanctuary, y church, z mosque" and so forth.

By hopefully accepting the fact that there is no limit to the development of the soul, one should try and define this duty towards oneself in such a way that it doesn't become a preoccupation or race against time, or again, the "development meter" type of thinking where you check it every day to see whether it's up or down or something like that. Development is limitless, an that is an encouragement rather than a sort of incentive to hurry and push and try and do too much

A person cannot judge how they feel and measure their spirituality and how they feel that their spirituality affects others in turn, except by their own reaction and feeling when face-to-face with themselves. It is a function of a teacher within the Tradition to judge this, to gauge it, to stimulate it, and to make available whatever he has at his disposal to help people in different circumstances, cultures or whatever; and this has to be done in a way that requires a very deep and latent cunning, because it must happen without the teacher letting himself be drawn into any discussion, estimation or even the smallest hint of a suggestion of an esoteric nature, along the lines of "Well, your soul doesn't seem to be going too well today." or something.

People try to get some sort of hint of this type back from me, I'll give them that, and they really do work at it. There's a sort of endearing Neanderthal spirit at large which pushes people to this sort of thing, and it's not to be decried because it's a normal level of understanding,

171

especially at the beginning. But you'll never get anything out of me on that level, that's for sure, because as I say, it is a definition which a person should, within reason, try to find for himself or herself. In this area there can be no definition of a conventional nature : for instance that it should be this size, this colour, this weight, and pointing North or South or anything like that.

So don't try and get a mental picture of it; rather try and get a mental picture of a relationship, of what the teachers have defined as to how this spirituality, this soul, can be nourished.

■

Chapter 17

Using the Tradition to deal with Negative Inner Reactions

How does one tackle, handle and generally overcome things like anxiety, fear, neurosis, complexes or any other phobia? This is not a psychological discourse : when I say how does one handle, look at them, get rid of or take care of them, I mean in the context of using techniques, instruments or other activities from the Tradition in order to do so.

Many people are familiar with what I have said about trying to distance oneself from problems and then look at them objectively, and then using a certain amount of energy to avoid repeating certain patterns of mistakes which people can have. Some use these tactics more usefully or regularly than others, yet there is another step before you use an exercise or an activity in this way, and that is to identify the area of the problem, hang-up or angst without going to the great lengths of detail that some psychiatrists or psychologists go to, that is regression and obscure influences.

The factors which apply during a person's lifetime may and certainly do influence people's reactions and feelings about certain things to a degree, if only because they develop a conditioned attitude or response towards these things. A certain amount of this conditioning is inevitable : it is imposed by social, religious, and other aspects of life. Again, a certain amount of this condition ing is perfectly valuable and reasonable, an without going too far, some preoccupations, problems or neuroses can be traced back to negative conditioning which a person has received.

There is another form of conditioning to which person is subject : and that is the conditioning which they impose upon themselves. In that a person is obviously and by definition present and close to himself or herself all the time, one's physical, emotional or psychic state of being is very much apt to be influenced by one's experience, mood or reaction at a particular time, under particular circumstances. The being is so closely knit that it is easy for an inner impact of one kind or another to have a greater influence on one's thinking, behaviour or reaction than another impact which comes from outside.

A person normally uses one technique or other in order to examine their reactions, and to protect and insulate themselves from certain impacts which they judge to be alien : these impacts can originate from people, outside circumstances, noise, heat, cold, hurry, worry; a thousand and one different messages are coming into a person on an hourly or daily basis. If a person is reasonably on guard, they will be able to prevent the majority of these negative impacts from disturbing them to any significant degree : the protection is there.

The insidious area of possible influence is the influence of people upon themselves. Let us say that in a particular kind of situation or circumstance, they have a certain reaction : good, bad or indifferent. Perhaps that reaction is generated by an outside circumstance exterior to themselves, or it may be that as a reaction to something which has come from the outside, their own deep reaction is of a nature which influences their thinking. You might say "This is perfectly obvious" : it is, but it is worthy of being examined, because this reaction or emotion can be fed to a person's being as a friendly feeling : it is not then subject to the same examination as an impact which comes so-called from outside. It has homogenized within the person.

A person's reaction to a situation or a circumstance with a lot of noise, hurry, bustle, people rushing about, may be one of anger or fear. Anger : "Why are these people rushing about? Why is there so much noise?" Naturally and deeply, something like discordant noise produces this sort of thing; a person's reaction is therefore one of anger or fear. Now maybe they take the usual step, which is to try and distance themselves from the noise, or else they look around and say "There's nothing to be actually afraid of." That is the first line of defense and they have gone through that tactic, right. However there is a possibility that a very small residue of anger or fear remains behind : and a few minutes or days afterwards when the person is in a completely different situation, he or she can happen upon this feeling of anger or fear, and very easily attach it to a circumstance in which they are at the time.

This is completely irrational, but it is a mechanical thing which does happen. Supposing there was a residue of fear or anger, and the person is in a situation which is neutral, neither good nor bad. If this residue of anger or fear surfaces, it can push, not the situation, but their attitude to the situation, in a different direction : "There is something about this situation I don't like, it makes me feel angry or afraid." This is what is called a false trace, but it does exist. You see the progression : if there is a residue of resentment, anger, fear, or something else left over from the old situation, it may surface hours, days, or weeks later in a situation which has no relation at all to the situation which first provoked it. Thus, in a normal situation which is neither good nor bad, it produces a feeling of frustration, anger, or resentment. A person is therefore under the impression that they have detected in the circumstance a reason for anger, fear or resentment, and they react accordingly.

So you have a completely irrational progression, but which can happen quite easily, and you have the domino phenomenon : a neutral situation, assessed by the person as being one which causes fear, aggression, anger : their reaction is then either fight or flee. If they fight, the ripples go out, and maybe they're fighting with another person or with a group of people who are then perhaps astonished by this person's outward behaviour towards them. They in turn react : "What is it to you?" and there you have the makings of a big conflict, with everybody stamping and storming out in all directions.

The other symptom may be one of fear : "There is some

reason why I feel unhappy in this situation, therefore this situation is one in which I should either flee from the fear or stop and get ready to defend myself." Of course if a person encounters a situation which stimulates fear, anger or resentment, it is also perfectly possible that the reactions they feel, the emotions which come to the surface, are not necessarily the result of some solidified trace which was left behind. What I am saying is that in areas where nervousness, anxiety, fear, aggression or anger is surfacing as a result of a false trace, what can one do about it, and how does one identify one from the other? Identifying the false trace from the real reaction is a fairly simple and obvious action. When one feels this feeling coming up, try and step back and look at it and see : "Am I touched? Am I influenced? Am I on the receiving end of something actually in the situation or could this possibly be something which I brought out myself? " This obviously has to be fairly quick thinking because if it is going to be a question of attack or defense, the decision has to be made very fast. The process has to be fast and clear ; one has to use the correct terms of reference.

If after literally a millisecond assessment of the situation one either reacts directly, or else if one has adequate reason to believe that this is a false trace coming to the surface, one should try and analyze the recent past to see where it may have started. Was there a situation in the recent past where this feeling was provoked? At that time there might have been an overt reaction, the person did something or said something and as far as they were concerned the situation was finished, but did it leave that false trace which is now coming up?

As I say, this is not a deep psychological or psychiatric examination : it is much simpler than that, it is also much cheaper. It does not involve stretching oneself out on a couch and being regressed back to the year dot. Most of these false traces are events which have happened in the recent past, that is a question of hours or days.

If one identifies an attitude or a reaction which is usually of a negative nature, i.e. fear, anger or resentment; when one has identified one of these false traces from the recent past, what does one do about it? To begin with, identifying it is more than half the battle. In order to remove it completely, wipe it out from the memory and don't just submerge it again because one then possibly allows it to bubble to the surface at some future occasion : you want to actually eradicate it.

The eradication or wiping out of such a trace is not as drastic as it sounds. It doesn't require some sort of catharsis, explosion, or terrible battle with oneself. Having identified it, if as is usual, it is of a negative nature, bring it into a reasonable and logical thinking area and give it some sort of measurement or name. You can give it any measurement, say it has a negative charge of two or five milli-amps or something like that : give it any sort of measurement that you like.

What then cancels out the negative potential? A greater and opposite positive. So, having brought the situation, the event, the feeling, out into the open as soon as possible, bring it clinically and clearly out into the open, keeping it in focus as if it was on the table in front of one; then focus a greater degree of positive potential onto it.

With such impacts, there is nothing spooky, extra-terrestrial and extraordinary about these traces which come up : they obey certain laws of physics, galvanism and physiology. The cerebral system and the nervous system work on a basic form of energy, which is a form of electricity. So in the practical sense, one is saying that in the case of these traces which people can easily magnify and make into perpetual hang-ups or deep neuroses or angsts : the vast majority of them can be overcome, or nullified and neutralized by a superior degree of the positive potential they already have available, because the system itself produces and feeds in the type of correct polarization that can wipe out these leftover residual traces which are left.

This technique can either be done in a general way, which has an element of overkill : one says "I feel that you're depressive, nervous, afraid or disconsolate about such and such a thing, therefore I will try and flood my whole system with positive potential in order to nullify this charge." This is perfectly feasible, but an element of overkill comes in here because if one can narrow down why, wherefore and how this all built up in a reasonable way, and get it into a reasonable focus, one can then try and direct energy of a positive nature towards it. You don't necessarily have to localize it in your left leg or your ear : if there is a situation, you focus on it, and by doing an exercise, by an activity, you produce enough energy to cancel it out.

You can of course very easily enable these personally produced preoccupations or hang-ups which verge on neurosis to become true neuroses by means of adequate retention : they flourish by attention and because they are able to influence a person. They use up more and more of a person's attention, but it is merely like blowing up a balloon. Substance? They have a minor substance : their only function is to distress, disturb, and generally molest a person.

So they are annoyances : you say "Well, forget about them" : no. Some you can forget about and you normally do so, they are expunged from memory in the normal process. For instance, today I was coming across Waterloo Bridge, and a car stopped beside another car, the car next to mine started off and as it accelerated away it gave an enormous and deafening backfire. I did not consciously concentrate on remembering the sound of that for ever and ever, but one progressively forgets such things, and this is a law and a very necessary one, otherwise the echoes of that incident would still be reverberating in my brain. Things decay naturally.

There is no reason why this natural potential for forgetting things usefully should not be employed in a way that prevents things from turning into the deeply-rooted well-nourished cultivated neuroses that people develop in spite of themselves. Some things, hopefully of a laudable nature, do remain with people : a sight, a sound, a tone, a fragrance, a place, a person : these are things which the person wants to remember, wants to be able to bring out, look at, file away, feel and so on. But there is no real need for people to collect, look after, bring out, polish up and put back all the little trials, tribulations, impacts, nervousness and preoccupations they collect so assiduously, and which are impacted on them all the time. In a normal human defense system, forgetfulness comes into operation automatically, autonomically.

How much better if one could harness and use this same system in a precise way for identifying, analyzing and neutralizing the impacts which one has nourished in spite of oneself. One doesn't want to nourish these things: who wants to remember a particularly nasty smell or situation? It's residual leftover is there, perhaps a person has thought about a particular nasty situation, and by thinking about it, has deepened its trace.

This is reasonable enough, because one says "Okay, I'd like to remember that, so the next time there is a similar situation, I won't fall into the same trap."That's fine, but only as long as it is kept as a sort of warning signal or reference, and not as "my preoccupation" or "one of my problems". It can easily develop into a pattern like that, and then these things roll up with each other, become a pattern of behaviour, and the angst becomes a prison of one's own making.

Everybody has the right to have an image of themselves : "I am this or that, I react to such and such a thing in this or that way" : this is reasonable enough ; one must have certain reactions, and one needs certain more or less fixed terms of reference, otherwise one would just be dithering about everything all the time : but this image that one has of oneself, whether sterotyped or deeply true, should not be an excuse for building an image which will let one down under certain circumstances.

Apart from any embarrassment which it might cause one, an attitude which leads to letting oneself down in a crisis simply erodes the image one has of oneself each time it happens. If you go to a grocer and one out of ten things you buy there are bad or rotten, your confidence in that grocer obviously diminishes and you finally go somewhere else : equally, one's confidence in oneself can be eroded until one says "Well I am just incapable of making any decision about anything, any time, because look at what I did last x, y, or z." Now if one looks at it logically and reasonably, this is simply not true : it is either laziness, evasion or stupidity which permits and encourages a person to so undermine themselves.

To a greater or lesser extent, everybody has some common sense on which they can build an image of themselves or the image of something positive. People do it all the time, let's call it one's "reliability rating" : one can rely on such and such a thing, person, or circumstance. If one is constantly building with one hand and sabotaging with the other, then the situation remains at best at a sort of zero and at worst it will be something which is getting lower and lower, at which point the classic neurosis comes into operation : "I can't make a decision, I can't trust myself to decide, I've asked so-and-so and they said this and I did that and it didn't work out, so I can't trust them either so I'll ask somebody else" : then you have "a-ring-a-ring of roses" situation, in which a person really can develop a good, sound, deeply-rooted neurosis based on their experience, on their emotional analysis of their own action, reaction or feedback.

All right, nobody is expected to be as unemotional as a stone, but people do have a responsibility towards themselves in that they should be accessible to themselves. They do have a responsibility to see that in the same way they choose the food that they eat, they have a responsibility to feed in the positive, good and useful feelings, and also produce something positive and useful.

People are so close to themselves that one can have an almost uncritical acceptance of what one thinks. You can feed yourself garbage : people do, frequently. They think "There, that's a good idea, it feels right" : it's garbage, but who is going to point at one and say "That is garbage!" : the reaction will be "No, that wasn't rubbish, it was a perfectly good idea, it was my idea, I thought it was brilliant" and they will defend it. They won't defend it because they are so sure it is not garbage, they will defend it as a matter of territorial integrity : "It is mine! My idea and I'll defend it." Justification then overcomes common sense and you'll see somebody standing with a drawn sword in front of a heap of rubbish prepared to give up their lives for their garbage.

What do you do? Well, you can hold up a mirror to them, actually that usually solves it, but it's better to prevent such a situation coming up later.

If you like, this is a side entrance to one's being. I should stress that it is not a side entrance which should be bolted, barred and defended, because there is a lot of good which is fed into it as well, but there should be an attempt to increase the vigilance over that area. When you have an unconditional acceptance of something "I thought of" : this unconditional aspect is always fraught not with possible danger, but with possible confusion. Let the acceptance be conditional : conditional upon my having examined it reasonably when I am in a reasonable frame of mind, when I am reasonably quiet, let me then perhaps go through it occasionally : it is what is known as examining oneself.

"Am I allowing a stream of garbage to go in? Do I believe everything I read in the Daily Telegraph?"The Daily Telegraph is written by people, with all that is good or bad in them. There are in fact a large number of lunatics who write for the Daily Telegraph. Even more of them who write for The Times, yet people say"Oh well, I read it in The Times!" : you will find millions of people who swear it must be true because they saw it in the Sunday Sport.

Unconditional acceptance can also be when it has such a ring of truth that you say "Well, I'm sorry, I am not capable or I don't have any wish to examine that" : now that happens rarely but it does exist. Conditional or reasonable examination is something you don't have to dissect down to the last molecule, because by doing that you will go down all sorts of side-alleys. Anybody who has gone into their attic or their cellar determined to clear it out knows exactly what I mean : after you've thrown away two things, you find an old scrap book and spend the rest of the day going through it, and by the time it's nightfall you think "Aha, I must start again tomorrow" and the same thing happens over again : so you can have over-dissection. At some point, when you're examining and allowing in a thing, you should get down to the basic material, and you should then be able to know whether it is in fact the basic material you are dealing with, so that you don't just go on for the sake of going on.

To sum up : you have to be very conscious of the fact that you can produce feeling and reaction within yourself which can form the building-blocks of what you might call your personality or your image. This is fine, but remember to examine them first. See if there are elements in them which bode ill for future reaction or future activities.

Try things out reasonably in the sense of the old system where you tap a thing and see whether it rings true. Do that within yourself : you can feed yourself garbage and accept it because you are say ing to yourself "It sounded reasonable, I thought of that." How many times have I heard people say to me "I thought it was a good idea at the time" : usually, it is that they really didn't think at all, they reacted. There are circumstances, times, situations where this sort of immediate reaction is necessary and laudable. There are also times when something has triggered off the idea that "Ah, I am a rational or educated x, y, z, therefore I ought to be doing this." The question is : should it be done? Is it a good thing, looked at from all points of view? Is one in a position where one is sabotaging one's own being or one's own effort by lack of thought?

■

Chapter 18

Belief

Questions are often asked about the position, attitude and relevance of the Tradition and its relationship with organizedreligion of whatever variety or persuasion. It might be useful to look at this, not in the sense of the religious study known as comparative religion, because usually a subject like comparative religion is just that, comparing one religious ethic with another, one term of belief with another, one pattern of worship or thought with another, and comparisons usually end up being odious.

When we look at the relationship between different organized religions and the Tradition, it is useful to examine certain fundamentals of religious belief. If one examines most religious beliefs without the million and one different interpretations, interpolations and attitudes, as far as man goes back it is clear that all religious belief from the beginning of time has in fact been unitarian and monotheist in nature. Confusion has been provoked by the people who either codified, interpreted, embellished or embroidered on what was the basic belief.

Going back to the Germanic or Nordic myths, you have these various Gods which make up a sort of Pantheon with Wotan and Freya, etc., and people say that from the dawn of Nordic or Germanic civilization, you had a pluralistic and polytheistic religious setup. They also say that if you look at the Hindu religion, you have their thousand and one different Gods, half-man, half-monkey, crocodile, cobra and so forth and so on : and then in the Christian religion you have the Catholic Trinitarian belief. Even if it is true that the Germanic or Nordic religion is no longer functioning as such; it did nevertheless occupy a very considerable time period : so how can I or the Tradition then claim that major religions are unitarian in character? How is it possible to say such a thing when one has three examples of a multitude of Gods or Goddesses, which is a polytheistic situation?

I believe this answer is worth considering, and it proves its own point, which is that if you examine the characteristics or nature of the different Gods and Goddesses and various other entities enshrined in these different religious systems, I think you will find that these different Gods and Goddesses, which have different characteristics, in fact represent different aspects of the same God.

You have Thor, the thunderer : this could be considered if you are drawn to the punitive, vengeful, jealous or threatening aspect : it is an aspect, right. You can then go through the Pantheon : you find Diana the huntress representing grace or beauty; again, another aspect. You have the sort of father figure, Wotan, yet another aspect. If you go through the Hindu Pantheon, you will find that the various Gods and Goddesses represent aspects of a character.

Just as in Islam we have various attributes of God which are not contradictory, but which are different aspects of a single being, a single entity : in our own small way we have different reactions, different points of view, different modes of behaviour, different attitudes. If you look at the Hindu Pantheon, you find that the territory in their Pantheon is well demarcated between Shiva and Kali and others : each one performs a distinct function. The demarcation lines are dropped : Kali is the Goddess of Death, whatever that implies. We are trying to go back to the origin, not to see what it is at the moment : at the moment Kali, the Hindu Goddess of Death, represents death, vengeance, and various other sordid things : human sacrifices were and possibly still are made to her in order that she should not manifest herself in undesirable form to people.

If you examine the different forms or characteristics in polytheistic belief, I think you will find that the particular characteristic embodied by one or other God or Goddess are aspects of what was originally a single Being. If one wants to go back to the dawn of time, say in a Stone Age situation, man was on the receiving end of all natural forces and natural calamities. This is something that can easily be seen in the Germanic or Norse myths : Thor the thunderer. When he was epitomized he was shown as the person with the gigantic hammer and when he struck, it caused thunder. You can easily see how a stone age man equated the power of nature, thunder and lightening andwhat was produced if lightening struck an object : this represented a primal force in nature to him. Gradually it was given a name, and it became Thor.

Now Thor had to be bought off, worshipped or placated so that he didn't strike a person down; therefore a temple was built, or else songs or verse or phrase was recited in his name. And then there was the Lord of the Deep, because somebody had to look after the fish and cause tides and cause people to be drowned or saved, and who other than of course a sea-god, Neptune? After all, somebody has to look after things : so this was very nice and tidy.

But there is a question here as well as an answer : the question is that before the threads of belief were drawn together, it was perfectly understandable and reasonable that primitive man should develop a Pantheon for himself: the God of the trees and vegetation, the God of the oceans, the God of hunting, the God of plenty, the God of the family, the God of the rocks and the God of the animals. I maintain that with the successive interpreters, interpolators or codifiers of religious belief in some very obvious cases like the Norse, the Germanic Gods and the Hindu Pantheon; that they did not codify these powers like water, air, earth, fire and so forth and say "These qualities of control over nature can be ascribed to one Being." There is no reason why not, firstly. And this is the real question : why, in some cases, was it not codified down to one entity? Now this may seem to be getting a little bit into the are of philosophical interpretation of religious belief : I think the answer is less philosophical and more a question of authority or power.

This is a loaded question and I'll give you a loaded answer : why have one temple for one God when you can have 75 temples for 75 different Gods, and all the authority, staffing and everything else which goes with it? If you have one temple for one Supreme Being, and you have four or five people looking after it, who perform or read the prayers or recite from the Holy Book or whatever : if there is a degree of self-interest or power-building, it is better that you involve as many people as possible : you will then have more people involved in worshipping your particular God of the day in a never-ending way.

Now this may seem to be a ridiculous and foolish situation. You might say "Why?" or "To what end?" or "In what interest?" This is a familiar phenomenon and there is a Nasrudin story about this : if you are excluded from or haven't got a place of pilgrimage because they're all taken, you start one up, and you staff it and look after it, and you get everything which goes with it. You may say this point of view is subjective : it certainly is controversial. I am speaking not only as a unitarian myself, but I am trying to explain why such misinterpretations came about, and whether they in fact have any relevance to religious belief, and to answer the question : where does the Tradition stand in relation to this?

If we go back to the beginning of any religious activity, it is maintained by all of the scholars, in the Tradition, and not just on the basis of blind faith : i.e. that because Islam is a unitarian religion, it must therefore be the same : no. From the point of view of how things come about, it is perfectly easy to see how, in the case of Islam, before Muhammed, there were 365 idols in the Kaaba in Mecca : one for each day of the year. They represented everything you can imagine : there was one idol for the boughs of the tree, one for the leaves of the tree, one for the trunk of the tree, and another for the roots of the tree.

If you were a farmer, you had to go to the Kaaba and pay

186

tribute or produce honey, water, silver, cloth or something like that for at least three or four separate Gods in
order to make sure that the roots, the trunk, the branch and
the leaves were looked after in your tree : then you
did further hocus-pocus to make sure there was rain
and locusts didn't get into it and things like that. So it was
a rather time-consuming activity, and it was also expensive
: it wasn't expensive for the people who ran the centre.

When Muhammad came on the scene, and during the
course of the establishment of the religion, you can very
clearly see that when the 99 names or attributes of God were
explained as being different qualities of a single God;
since Muhammad did away with the 365 idols, how easily
at that point 99 idols could have been created, each one
representing an aspect of God. What I maintain is that at
this point of development, there could have been a replay
of what happened in the old Norse myths or in the Hindu
religion.

One of the fundamental reasons why it is so important
to clarify this point is that, if one is functioning and living
in the Tradition, at the same time as one is trying to develop a deeper knowledge of oneself and of one's being,
one is then hopefully being led to a point where one's
relation-ship with or where one stands with regard to God
is clarified. If you are in a situation where you have a
diffusion of your attention, in which we have to, say, try
and work out a relationship with or placate 99 different
Gods at the same time, this would literally be very difficult. It is perfectly reasonable and plausible to realize that
all and every one of the functions or aspects which are
delegatedtothedifferent Norse, Germanic, and Hindu
gods can all be encompassed in one individual Being, if one
believes at all in the existence of God. If He is indeed, and
one accepts that He is the Creator of the Universe, then all
of the powers represented by any of the hundred thousand
Hindu Gods, or the Germanic or Norse or other Gods, can
be under His control.

There is no question about this , nor can we imagine that
there would be any, because if one brings it out and looks

at it clearly, I venture to suggest that this is the only scenario which is useful. How does that then relate to the Catholic or Trinitarian belief? I think there is no confusion. In the broad outlines of the Catholic Church, whether Catholic or Protestant, you have the Bible and you have the two main books, the New and Old Testament. The Old Testament was completed in some thing like 390 B.C., and the first book, Matthew, of the New Testament in something like 38 A.D.

The original versions of the Old Testament certainly use phrases which could be interpreted as definitely indicating a Trinitarian situation : the Father, the Son and the Holy Ghost. Now one's examination of religious belief can and should be similar to the way one would examine oneself : it does not necessarily imply that the examination should be of a hostile nature. If one examines a thing, one examines it to a purpose of understanding it better or learning about it in order to use it or reject it.

The Christian or Catholic Trinitarian thesis is unusual in the sense that almost all of the recognized accepted religions prior to Christianity were of a unitarian nature. Zoroastrianism, although it later degenerated into a sort of Cabalistic system, was basically unitarian. But if one reads the Old Testament and the New Testament carefully, you will find that there are certain interpretations placed on certain sayings which, as I say, would give basis to a Trinitarian thesis. I don't think there is really a source of confusion, and there certainly isn't a source of conflict : the phrases which are cited to justify the Trinitarian system are perfectly acceptable to a non-Catholic, given that God is considered to be Creator of all things and all life; therefore going back to the original version, as a Creator He could and is considered to be the father of all things.

If you personalize it into the "person of Jesus" you get into deep waters. The question of the Holy Ghost : this entity is also mentioned in Islam in the Koran, and, as I say, there is no area of conflict. My only concern is that I think it is more useful to go back to essentials, the basis of things. This in no way should be considered critical of the Trinitarian situation, and I shouldn't be quoted as meaning that.

Belief

Does one reject Jesus, does one reject the Holy Ghost? Not at all. What one does take issue with, and what one can look at and wonder about, is whether this development and interpretation of the basis of the Christian religion is necessary : and it is indeed interpretation and development. Is it necessary, how does one relate to it, or does one?

It is not a question of saying "Well I will reject this" : we're not in the business of rejecting or accepting. What we are doing is trying to go back to certain known and basic factors, which one can feel, and then increasing in that way the relationship with such factors, leaving aside the unnecessary.

When I say the unnecessary, this is not a direct or veiled criticism or accusation against any faith, because Islam or Judaism or Christianity have had plenty of additions, accretions, embroidery, interpretations and mis-interpretations over the centuries. At this very moment you have the tussle in Islam between the so-called "Fundamentalists" who claim to be the real voice of Islam, and who have produced an "Imam" and so forth, and you have the vast majority who are true fundamentalists, who work and behave in a fundamental way based on the beliefs, and who don't make a big song and dance about it.

Over the centuries, since no one can actually be immediately disproved by direct reference to God : "Excuse me God, is he telling the truth?" : a lot of people have and will write all sorts of books, create all sorts of theories, and do all sorts of things.

But why not say "All right, the way I should worship God doesn't really preoccupy me, providing I do so. The technique does not particularly preoccupy me, providing I use one. I should not be in the business of comparison : "So-and-so was first, therefore he was better" and so forth and so on". We have certain terms of reference, yardsticks and measurements, and they boil down to the function of belief, not just belief as an abstract, not just "Believe? Oh yes, I believe." Examine what one does believe, how it relates to one, how one uses it, otherwise it's abstract. "Are you a believer? Yes, I'm a believer" : well, justify your belief. It's a thing which one feels, which one works on, not to persuade one to believe, but to examine how and when one has believed and in which cirrcumstances, and to relish those circumstances, and examine them, again, as proof of belief : so they can say to you "Believe!" and you say "Right, I believe."

Believing is fundamental to human beings : they need something to believe in : a cause, a religion, a belief. And it doesn't help them one bit to read four hundred books of the religious philosophy of their belief, unless they are themselves making, keeping, nourishing and enhancing the contact between them selves and the source of their belief

There is no useful function in merely having a label as something : "I am a Dervish, I am a Sufi." Nobody is going to challenge you, and say "Prove it!" How does a Dervish prove that he is a Dervish? He goes round carrying a kashkul and wearing a tattered robe and sitting under a palm tree? Anybody can do that. How does he prove that he is a Sufi? What do Sufis look like? "I saw a Sufi once, he didn't look anything like you." Well, that is no measure. The proof of a person being a Dervish rests within themselves and their relation to the Tradition.

You have to hold onto a central belief. It is perfectly reasonable and normal to be brought up and educated in a religious system : I'm not saying for a moment that at this stage or at this moment one should start questioning or throwing away tracts or books. But one must hold on, one can't debase it : there cannot be a Dervish without belief. There cannot be a Sufi without the central pillar of the belief. Upon this, a Dervish or a Sufi builds.

One can perfectly well discuss or compare religious theory or belief, or even dispute such matters, as long as it is done in a reasonable and amicable way.

There is no good or bad religion : there is only a bad state, which is absence of belief. Absence of belief is absence of a fundamental pillar of existence. There are many different ways and forms in which this is manifested : as I say, one can then get into the area of the comparative, which is a never-ending source of anguish and confusion. It is the quality of the belief which is important, not the quantity, and it is the strength of the belief which produces an answer to the belief.

So we do not seek out a good, better or best religion. The fundamental point is that there should be one, and the central point of whichever belief is involved is the belief in one Being.

The paths and the roads to, the form of worship to, the embroidery on every aspect of it, is and has been a pastime, and much blame actually can be lain at the door of both Western and Eastern philosophers who have misinterpreted these matters for whatever reason, and who have encumbered and created obstacles for people, such as tests : tests of belief, tests of this, that and so forth. In fact a person tests themselves. They do not need the established religion or Church to judge and test them; they are their own severest critic in terms of their belief. They cannot and should not seek to hide away from themselves.

Too much religious zeal and enthusiasm can produce results that are perhaps extraordinary : people can have all sorts of experiences and visions which they can then interpret according to certain fixed measures within their own religion. There is a step before that, and the step is to see whether this experience or vision is, in fact, real, or whether it is a product of their imagination or over-enthusiasm.

■

Chapter 19

Questions and Answers :
Religion, Death, God and Predetermined
Destiney in the Context of the Tradition

Spiritually and physically, if we maintain solidarity and unity, it does not always mean that we will be physically safe from difficulties. It does mean, however, that those of us in difficulty will have the support of every brother and sister in the Tradition : because if any member or group in the Tradition suffers problems, we all react together. We do not all suffer together, but we send our positive energy to those who are having problems, and with that quantity of actual energy, we can help them to overcome them. This may not make it easier for them to solve their problems as such, but it does mean that they recover from their problems much more quickly.

We are a brotherhood, a sisterhood, a family : touch one, and you touch us all. There may be some who at one time or another are more vulnerable, who may occasionally suffer more, but I will give you two guarantees : not promises, because I don't deal in promises, fairy stories and exaggerations : it's simply that if and when we do send our united energy to friends who have problems, their problems and the after-effects involved will be less.

There is one function of responsibility I want to mention within the Tradition. Responsibility in the Tradition is one which every person takes on themselves. One is respons-ible for making the effort to understand, and one is also responsible for trying to explain to others what they have understood; but one must be careful that one has oneself properly understood before one explains, otherwise it can become an interpretation and not an understanding, and you get the interpretation of the interpretation. In the Tradition one of the very important functions of the older members is to communicate.

There is no authority without responsibility. The longer a person has been in the Tradition, the greater their responsibility to explain to people who come in newly. Everybody has similar questions, similar doubts. If one feels that it is always possible to ex-plain the doubts to some other person, one will find that this person will very often say "Yes, I had the same feelings, the same questions, or the same doubts." One can then say "Do this or do that, or think like this or think like that." Or else one can say: "In that situation, or with that problem, I did this, that, or the other." The answer lies somewhere in between the two.

To give precise advice to a person, you must know that person totally. It is the responsibility of every more experienced member to know the people in his or her group. If I ask one of the more experienced members about somebody, or about their problems or questions, I do not want to hear : "I don't know about them." To use authority you must understand authority : to give orders you must learn to take orders.

Contact is the most important thing. Contact does not mean that everybody is responsible for every action of everybody else. Contact means that they know if there is a problem or a question that exists. It also means choosing the time and the way to speak or help that person. If one is careful in usual and normal social situations, it is perfectly possible and necessary within the Tradition to talk to and communicate with somebody, and to choose the correct time and technique. If you think that a friend has a doubt or a problem, and for instance you have coffee with them and talk to them, you create a situation of communication and rapport. I hope you do not invite them to coffee and sit behind a desk with a white coat and a notebook : that technique also has a place. Again, not one extreme or the other, somewhere balanced in the middle.

What everybody should learn is not only how to do something, but when. I will decide to do something in one hour, but in one hour a situation changes, so I must modify my technique according to the time element. A person learns by feeling the time and the situation. If a person is in a particular situation, one can look at it and say "I remember a similar situation and I did that thing" and then one does it, and it turns out a disaster. They then doubt the technique, doubt themselves, they examine themselves, the situation, the technique, find a similar situation, and do the same thing over and it's a disaster again. The situation is the same, the question is the same, the problem, the people, the place are the same : the time is different.

One day, Nasrudin was going home from the Friday prayer, and he was feeling a little sad and depressed, and he came to an old graveyard, and he saw an old open grave. He had been thinking: "I wonder what death is like." So he got into the grave and lay down, and he lay there and watched the clouds pass over; it was very calm and quiet. He stayed there for about fifteen or twenty minutes. While he was lying there a man had brought some camels into the graveyard to graze on the grass, and Nasrudin thought, "Oh well, I'd better go home" so he jumped out of the grave, and frightened all the camels. The man who was looking after the camels took a big stick and beat him.

Nasrudin went home and he was late for lunch and his wife was very angry with him for being late, and he said: "Don't be angry because I was experiencing what death must be like." She became very interested, and said, "That's very interesting, what is death like?" Nasrudin said: "Well, it's very nice, very calm; you see the clouds passing by, and it's very tranquil and lovely. There's only one problem : if you frighten the camels, they beat you."

That is one interpretation of death. You could have a situation where people hear that story, and they leave out the bit about getting beaten. If the story is shortened, then the explanation is that Nasrudin said that death is very nice and quiet and you lie there and you watch the clouds, finish. So you can have over-interpretation and you can have under-interpretation. It is better to have no interpretation at all.

Sufism for Today

*

According to the traditions and laws of Islam, Muhammad was the seal of the prophets, or the last prophet. One must clearly understand the relationship between Islam, the Tradition and Christianity, and this raises another question. When the Koran and the traditions of Islam refer to Mohammed as the last prophet or seal of the prophets they automatically indicate that Islam recognizes and accepts the Prophet and all former prophets, including Jesus. We don't really need to get into a long and involved discussion as to the claims of one religion, as to the identity of their founder or their leader, and with the validity of the authority of the founder or any other position: let us leave that sort of thing to professional debaters. There is no question of the validity of each scripture, whether it be the Torah, the Bible, or the Koran. The context, message and values were all similar. So, for the attitude or relationship between the Tradition and Christianity, the answer is that there is a relationship, and there is no competition, there is no problem, there is no conflict or criticism.

Equally, if one accepts the prophets as having been, which they undoubtedly were, great teachers; there should be no competition between them. Professional theologians can invent and produce areas of conflict between the different religions : it is their profession to do so; without theological discussion they would be out of a job. The question of the validity of various religions is not really basic, because one is examining the fundamental, commonly-held roots in all religions and beliefs. If we get down to the basic teachings of the great teachers of the past, we find a common heritage : they were orthodox in the most correct sense of the word. If it is true that they spoke and shared a basic source of truth, then I can say one thing: I am more Catholic than the Pope.

As far as whether one should either expect another prophet, or whether the established religions, the last of them being fourteen hundred years old, have lost momentum or become worn out, the answer to both questions is no. If they appear to have become worn out or to have

196

lost their momentum, the fault lies not with the religion, but with the people whose function it was to update it constantly. If, at any period, they lost the spirit of the message and took to the letter of the message, they lost momentum.

The technical observances of different religions can be updated and adapted without having to make a compromise. Certainly, the quality and character of a religion should hold and maintain its place in a developing society. By that, I don't mean that one should necessarily have jukeboxes and snack bars in cathedrals or mosques to attract the public, because in my experience, it is the ambiance and the character of the cathedral, synagogue or mosque, and the character of the person in charge of it, which attracts the people, and not the neon sign or the Bingo. If one holds to the basic aim and values of a religion, its shape and form in a developing society can easily be established. This has to be done carefully and well, and by professionals.

There is a real danger that a place of worship, synagogue, church or mosque can lose its place in a people's culture, because if it becomes a monument to old beliefs it can lose its impetus and momentum. If it relies on its superstitious and monumental character for its validity, it will die. If it maintains and develops a place not only in the culture of the people but in the hearts of the people, then it will develop and continue to be functional. The function of a building sanctified for worship is also a place of security and peace, at least that's what it should be, but too many times it becomes an empty monument to dreams.

Within the last fifty years, many priests of different denominations and religions have tried to update their image. Some have hired public relations agencies to make people care for them more; some have put on leather jackets and jeans, have grown their hair down to their bottoms or had their teeth capped. Why the need for a "swinging" approach if what you are saying is valid? Surely, if you are talking and transmitting to people on many levels, and you're speaking to their hearts : why should you seek to attract them by their eyes?

Certainly, people can and should use different ways of attracting and holding attention, I do it myself. But if I keep on trying to attract attention by only the visual impact I make, after a certain time that visual impact wears off. Using artificial means to attract and hold attention can only work in an artificial context. The people who feel the need of playing guitars in the pulpit and wearing jeans in order to be "with it" don't give enough credit to the common sense feeling which everybody has.

Everybody everywhere, at some time or another in their lives, is searching. Very often, they don't know exactly what it is they are looking for, but they feel very deeply that in their lives, in their existence, there is something missing. If they decide what they are looking for at the outset, there is a possible danger that they will make a conditioned choice, that is, they set out with the idea : "I want to find a particular philosophical system, a particular esoteric tactic or supernatural experience" and they may very well find it.

It may be correct for them. But a lot of other people are helped in their search by a feeling for something. They cannot define what that feeling is; they know when they find it. They know what they need. They know what they find when they find it, and they know by what is called, if you like, a sixth sense, an inner feeling.

What has this got to do with the Church or religion developing or holding a place in human society? What it has to do is very simple, because from religion and belief comes a developmental philosophy within and beyond religion. A complete religion is basically composed of two aspects : the practical or historical, and the philosophical or esoteric teaching. Usually the function of the activities, the history and the tradition of a religion introduce a person to the philosophical or esoteric teaching. For various reasons, the esoteric, hidden or secret meanings of religion ave sometimes been deliberately removed. This can be one of the reasons why it can appear that a religion is decaying in influence and losing its impetus : because the "introductory" function of the religion has been cut at the point where it could take off.

Questions and Answers

The first process prepares for the second; the first process without a second will either decay or turn round and round on itself like some form of philosophical chewing gum : after a while it loses its taste but you go on chewing because it has become a habit. Very often, people will continue through the first processes of religion and repeat those processes over again in the belief that it will lead them to something they know exists. They are understandably not enthusiastic about leaving the religion in which they have been born, which may have the sam chewing-gum effect.

People, for instance, might leave Christianity to go to Islam or from Christianity to Judaism or any other permutation, because they have heard that there exists a developmental or secret teaching in another religion. The truth is, of course, that there is a hidden content, a secret teaching in all of the great religions. If it is not fully functioning, it is usually because certain aspects of it have been deliberately suppressed.

You might think that this is a very serious allegation to make against many generations of priests of different denominations. I make this accusation against some people who were in positions of authority, not all, and I would consider that their motivation for doing what they did was because they wanted to maintain a domination over people. The esoteric or secret content of a religion aims at the liberation of that person from any form of domination by helping their inner development.

If you happen to be a priest, and you don't understand the real function of the hidden teaching, you might consider that this is aimed at your authority. You might think that this would take people away from the functions of established religion, that this philosophical or esoteric teaching might replace the established religion in people's lives and hearts : this is not true. The basic functioning of the Church within society : to christen, to marry, to bury, to be a sanctuary, to be a centre of worship, has a valid place in every society.

In a philosophical or esoteric context outside the formal

church situation, you can have esoteric experiences. But if you ask a reasonably average young person whether they would rather have an esoteric experience or get married, I don't think you would get very many votes for esoteric experiences. Religions, if they are the original religions complete in their totality, do not have a decay factor.If they have been changed and modified out of all recognition, then they can and do have a decay factor.

*

I have been asked about death, and one's reaction to it.The answer is to react in a useful way. Understandably enough, death has emotion connected with it. I'm not saying that in the face of somebody's death, one should not show one's emotion; it's the normal and natural thing to do. But if one really looks at one's reaction correctly, one will find that most of the emotion is for oneself. One is sorry for oneself because one has lost a friend, somebody one loves, and one loses the physical contact with that person. Yes, it is a loss and one is sad.

A person is as dead as one considers him or her to be. If they continue to exist in the memories and in the hearts of people, if one remembers them with humor and affection, they are absent; they are not dead. Of course it depends, again, whether one considers that death is lying in a hole in the ground, or if it is part of an ongoing pro cess of human existence. In the event of a person's death, usually in the Tradition, his family or his friends would hold a meeting two or three weeks after his passing, for coffee or tea or drinks or dinner or whatever, and this to remember him or her, and talk about them with humor and with kindliness : and you keep them in your memory as a present person.

You don't go to an extreme and consider them as a sort of ghost wandering about in the house, nor to any other extreme. You mourn their passing, you're sorry for the loss of the contact, but you keep their memory alive.

*

Questions and Answers

What is fear, and how can it be controlled or eliminated ?

The simple and very short and clear answer is : with faith. The practical application of this belief and faith and confidence in something must be known in the application of this faith, belief or confidence; and how it can be applied should also be known.

How does one apply techniques from the Tradition in the correct way to do this? When I say correct, I mean at the right time and positively. Any technique, any call for help or aid when one is afraid should be a positive action and not a superstitious reaction. A simple, useful and powerful protection against the buildup of fear is to call upon some energy to help you in this situation. This energy has to come from some source, a person, a place or even a context or an ambiance. In a time of fear or difficulty, which after all is usually a negative emotion, the tactic is to flood the consciousness with the positive.

If you are faced with some actual fear, or you have a number of vague fears, and in the face of those fears you feel weak or vulnerable, it is no shame to call for assistance. After all, in a physical situation of fear and danger, if you are menaced by somebody or a number of people, you call your friends or the police to help you. When the fears are perhaps vague but still menacing, call a person : imagine strongly or vividly a place or context which is highly positive to you personally. Take that positive energy and use it against the negative fear. Whichever person or place or context is the most positive and the strongest to you : use that.

It may not always be the same energy, but it should be a person, place or context which is familiar to you. It should not be something strange or with which you feel a little bit uncomfortable. If you're going to use this positive charge, you have to use it strongly and with determination, not with semi-hesitation : "Shall I use it, can I use it? Do I have the right to use it? Is this a negative enough situation that I can use it?" The broad answer is yes, one can use this tactic for all circumstances where fear exists.

If it is a sort of general fear of the unknown, you either find out what it is and it becomes known, or you decide that since it is unknown and vague it cannot have much influence on you. Look at your fears, examine them and try and chase them back and see where they come from .

*

God, and what is the maximum nearness which a person can achieve to Him?

This question is really not fair, because a lot of people have written endless numbers of books about this. Since the question itself is really not fair, I will cheat a little on the answer : let me say what can God be to a person.

Now a person can certainly take God as a context and put and keep God in a position of great height and power. There is no debating that God is in a position of great height and great power. But how does man relate to God? With the help of books and texts which exist in the Tradition, a person should try and develop what I might call a personal idea of God. I recommend the reading of various books and manuscripts from the great masters, because in one way or another, directly or indirectly, they help a person to develop this personal view. Another aid is a publication which gives the ninety-nine names or Attributes of Go : this book immediately gives one an idea of the total extent of the being of God.

A person cannot or should not therefore decide that God is terrible, because that means he has one attribute. If you decide that God is only terrible or jealous or vengeful, your attitude and reaction will be based on something very close to fear. Certainly it might be a help if you say: "I'd better not do this thing because God will punish me for that. "If any feeling prevents you from doing something which is negative towards yourself or somebody else, this is certainly beneficial. But are you behaving in that way, i.e. avoiding an error, because you are afraid, or is it because you don't want to make that error? It should be more the second and not the first.

If a person says to you: I think it is better for you to do this thing rather than that thing, you certainly have a choice. You can continue with the errors, or you change for a more beneficial attitude. Say the person just said to you : "It will be better for you to leave that and do this." It's not better because "I want you to do it", or" I order you to do it" or I threaten you that if you don't do it, this will happen.

In the various scriptures and revelations which He has sent to mankind, God has commanded, He has ordered. But at the same time He has specified and indicated aspects of His character which are merciful. Sheikh Omar Khayaam in the Rubayyat has a verse about this. He says that one day there was a man who was complaining to God, and he said "Oh God, you created me with all the faults which I have, are you going to punish me for these faults, or is the fault yours for creating something faulty?" The answer to that, of course, lies in the range of qualities which God possesses.

One can say "That's all very nice, but if I do something, how do I know what mood God is in at that moment? Is He being merciful or is He being vengeful?" So you either don't do anything, or else you take the risk. However, if you have clearly looked at the situation and the context in which you are acting, you should be able to get an approximate idea, because if one is going to do something and the end result is going to be negative for oneself or somebody else, it doesn't take very much philosophical examination to decide that, as a result, one is going to get a problem.

That doesn't mean that one rushes about fearfully looking back over one's shoulder, expecting to get bashed at any moment. Most often, the person who does the punishing and the person who suffers is the person himself. If you go up to a door and you take a stone and you break the glass in the door, God correctly does not suffer or get unhappy. What usually happens is that the person whose door it is comes out and punches you in the eye. Now you shouldn't consider that punch in the eye as some sort of Divine Vengeance.

A person looks for God, seeks God, and progressively fills in what he or she considers to be the nature of God. There are obviously certain indications or influences of a personal nature which a person uses to try and define the nature of God. A person can be influenced by what they would like God to be. Argentinos would like God to be an Argentino : women would like God to be a woman. I am sure that God is an Afghan, but that is my personal idea.

When trying to approach God one does not make a decision that God is in apartment number 72, 352 meters up, because you can spend your whole life building a tower exactly to that altitude. Since He is God and He has the total authority, by the time you have built the tower He might have moved, so you start all over again. To get close to God, you start to try and develop an understanding of the nature of God.

If a person can try as hard as possible to behave in ways which are harmonious to the Attributes of God, that person does not become God, but he or she can share in the entity of God. As I say, one shouldn't start feeling and believing that one is God, but if one considers that God views humanity with His own particular characteristics which are His Attributes : supposing we consider that God enjoys His various attributes. Therefore if we can try and develop areas of similar quality, surely then we could start developing the same contentment that God has in His Attributes.

*

Destiny is a context. Now, you can quote any number of people, authors, poets, who have said Destiny is destiny, what is written is written, man cannot avoid destiny, etc. If that is so, that a person's destiny is written and decided at birth, there's another question, and that is what is the purpose of life? If certain experiences or situations are pre-determined and I can't do anything about them, what is the purpose of life?

The analogy of the purpose of life is really very simple. Life is a voyage. Supposing we accept for the moment that you have a point of birth and you have a person's destiny, and between the two there is the voyage, the road. It is not in fact as simple as that, because after all, it is the voyage, the travelling that is important, and not arriving at this destiny.

Take again the analogy of the voyage, of the journey : a man leaves his home to take up a job in another country; say he is a carpenter. When he leaves his home he doesn't have his tickets to get to his destination, he doesn't have all the money to pay his expenses on the way. So he travels a little way, meets people and compares points of view. He arrives at a village, he doesn't have very much money, so he works at a trade, which is being a carpenter. And in that six months, one year, or three years that he stays in that village, he develops his skill as a carpenter. He has saved a little money, so he moves on his journey.

He meets people, visits other countries, and he broadens and increases his experiences. And he arrives at another town or village, and again, he works at his carpentry and develops his carpentry skill. So he goes on, he travels, he learns about travelling, he learns about other people. He also learns a lot about himself; how he reacts to certain problems, certain situations. Finally when he arrives at his destination or his destiny or whatever, he is a better person and a better carpenter. If, at the place of his destiny, there is a place for a master carpenter, he can fit in. He could not have fitted in to that position when he started out, if he had gone directly. Therefore, he has travelled, he has learned, he has developed himself, and he is better able to benefit from whatever in that destiny is his.

People can travel and arrive at their destination empty-handed, or they can arrive with something which will benefit them in that place which they call their destiny. Between those two points a person is a free man. He can travel until his money is exhausted, and then he can steal a chicken and eat it : say he continues to do this, it's no problem, it's easy to steal, and he develops a habit of doing it. In whose hands is the responsibility for the stealing? Is it the man who let his chicken run freely without watching over it? Is it God, who decided "Well I suppose today I might as well let him steal a chicken or something? " Or is it the decision of the man based on his own greed and laziness? You might say it was his hunger or his need, but did he go to anybody in a village and knock on a door and say : "I am hungry? " Or did he take the easy way, which became a habit destructive for him because he learned nothing except to steal?

Not only that, but by stealing a chicken, or a goat, or a loaf, he has probably created circumstances. Does he know or does he care that stealing that chicken, goat or loaf means that a family will go hungry? Does he know that if that family is starving, that the father of the family will not go out and find food? Does he know or care that if the father doesn't find the food and is desperate, he might steal food? Does he know or care that the father could be arrested and jailed? Does he know or care that the children of that family will blame the political or social system when they grow up and become rebels, revolutionaries, reactionaries, or whatever; and will then cause confusion, death, war, or anything else? The falling of governments, international war : all because one man was greedy and lazy and stole one chicken?

Hopefully, international war and famine does not start every time somebody steals a chicken, but the impacts of one's actions should be considered. If a person is travelling in a train, and they're drinking a can of beer and throw the can out of the window, as far as they're concerned their relationship with that can is finished : there was a can, they had beer, they drank it, they don't need the can, therefore they throw it away; but the falling of that can could start a whole chain of circumstances. One should always try to be conscious as to the possible ongoing impacts of one's act-ions, in a balanced way.

You do not have to go around thinking : "Shall I light this cigarette, shall I drink this coca-cola, or is it possible that I might start a World War?" That is a recipe for neurosis, and people are neurotic enough. But in areas where there is a possible spin-off, a person has a responsibility to themselves and to others to be careful.

■

GLOSSARY

Abjad : System of Arab numerology which makes use of the Arabic language's unusual flexibility in linking the linguistic roots of words to both numbers and philosophical concepts. For fuller account, see pages 110-112 and 173-181 in THE SUFIS by Idries Shah (Octagon Press, London).

Arif : Gnostic or person who has gnosis, i.e. direct knowledge of the Divine Reality. The word for gnosis is marifah (see **marifah**).

Asma : The name, as in " al-asma al-husna" or the 99 Most Beautiful Names of God. These names or attributes are divided into Names of Essence and Names of Quality. The latter are divided into Names of Majesty, which have to do with rigor, and Names of Beauty, which have to do with compassion.

Ayn al-Qalb : the eye of the heart, which refers to the Spirit's eye which sees the Real (al-Haq) when it is unveiled, otherwise this eye is veiled and has no vision of God and transcendental realities. The primary concern of the Sufi Tradition is to purify this inner eye of the heart.

Auliya or Abdal : A person within whom a qualitative change has taken place at soul or spirit level, which is the original meaning of "Saint".

Baraka : Special grace, blessing or benediction. Beings or things can contain baraka i.e. Abdals, holy places, objects, positively-intentioned deeds, certain rituals & exercises, etc.

Batin : The inward or inner, as in al-Batin or The Interior, one of the 99 names or attributes of God. The word " batini" means esoteric, and " ilm al-batin" means the science of the inward, or esotericism.

207

Bayat: Act of commitment by the Sufi towards his teacher. It is a pact between Master and disciple which engages both parties, and implies rebirth and entry into the Path. It is said to confer the grace and power that will then have to be brought out by the efforts of the pupil: this rite is considered to have been transmitted from the days of the Prophet and is restricted to those who follow the Sufi Path.

Bismillah : The beginning or " Fatiqa" of the Koran : "Bismillah al-Rahman al-Rahim" (In the name of God, the Compassionate, the Merciful). It is the formula used to consecrate all deeds when one begins them, just as "al-Hamdullila" is used when an action has been brought to an end.

Dervish : Another word for a Sufi. The word has been incorrectly used in the West to designate a religious fanatic or to denote obsessive activity.

Exercise : Any prayer, recitation or spiritually intended evocation that has been specifically assigned to an individual or group by the teacher. Exercises are only performed under the guidance of a teacher, and not at the initiative of a disciple.

Ghaflah : Forgetfulness, not just as a memory lapse, but as a psycho-physical veiling of the heart. Ghaflah feeds the momentum of the Fall (see al-Hubut) and causes the dispersal of attention that prevents, among other things, the proper performing of an exercise.

Hadith or Traditions : A statement by the Prophet Muhammad, or an eyewitness or near-eyewitness account of one of the Prophet's actions. They are for the most part the Prophet himself speaking, and should not be confused with the Divine Revelation as expressed through Muhammad in the Koran. This material was collected soon after the Prophet's death, and the traditionists Al-Bukari and Muslim laid down a sophisticated historiographical framework for sifting out any doubtful or invented stories from the Prophet's life, which effectively prevented this material from becoming mythologized by succeeding generations. The six authoritative collections are those of Al-Bukari, Muslim, Abu Dawud, Al-Tirmidhi, Al-Nasai and Ibn Maja.

Much of this remarkable material has never been translated into English.

Hijra : The emigration from Mecca to Medina by the Prophet and his small band of followers in 622 A.D. which is the year I of the Hijra in the Muslim calendar.

Hubut : The Fall from the Garden of Eden, implying loss of the primordial state through veiling of the heart. The recovery of the Edenic state lies through the inner purification of the heart, which will allow the contemplative to see the transcendent realities perceived by Adam before the Fall. In Islam, the Fall is immediately followed by the revelation given to the redeemed Adam, who is the first in the line of God's Prophets and Messengers that culminate in Muhammad.

Imam : In the time of the Prophet, an Imam was a man or woman who lead the congregation in prayer. A cult has grown up among the Shia which has turned the Imam into a kind of clergy-cum-political commissar : this is expressly contradicted by the hadith stating that there should be no priesthood or monkery in Islam.

Kashkul : A kind of elongated bowl, often symbolically decorated, which is sometimes made out of certain types of gourd. It is often hung in a group's Tekkia or Exercise Chamber, and it is historically associated with Dervishes because it was used as a begging-bowl when Dervishes were sent out to beg as an exercise in humility.

Marifah : Gnosis or the direct knowledge of Divine Reality that comes from pursuing the spiritual Path. It implies a perfected wisdom or experiential knowledge, which should be distinguished from the ordinary theoretical knowledge, that is a purely mental phenomenon. The aql or intellect is involved in both ways of thinking, but in gnosis the intellect is situated in the heart whereas in theoretical knowledge it is situated in the brain : in the first it is intuitive, in the second it is discursive.

Mathnavi : The poetical and philosophic masterpiece of the 13th-century poet and Sufi Jalaludin Rumi, who founded the Mevlevi Order of Dervishes in Konya. The Mathnavi has been called " The Bible in Persian".

Murshid, Murshida : More experienced or senior member of a Sufi group, who is expected to provide guidance and help to newer members.

Nafs : the soul or psyche; also the ego or commanding self. In the sense of soul, it means the reality of man that is the intermediary between the spirit (ruh) and the body. The soul is saved or damned at the hour of death through judgement, the body being left behind until the Day of Resurrection. In the sense of ego, it opposes the operation of man's spirit by dulling its radiance and preventing it from shining through.

Naib : Teacher's deputy, who will normally administer and coordinate activities in a given area or country on behalf of the teacher, and who will liaise between disciples and teacher.

Nasrudin : Traditional " wise idiot" folk-hero who has become part of oral folklore throughout the Middle East. He has always been associated with the Sufi Tradition and is often used by teachers to exemplify both positive and negative ways of thinking. See the *EXPLOITS/ SUBTLETIES/ PLEASANTRIES OF THE INCREDIBLE MULLA NASRUDIN* by Idries Shah, ed. The Octagon Press, London.

Qalb: The heart or subtle organ of knowledge or feelings, synonymous with the inner spirit of Intellect. When veiled by the effect of ghaflah or forgetfulness, it becomes dominated by passions and ignorance. Its purification through the interior " jihad" or holy war, is part of the Sufi Path, and leads to the unveiling of the " eye of the heart" or " ayn al-Qalb" which means that the Spirit triumphs over the negative tendencies of the soul.

Qutub or Pillar: One of the Four High Authorities of the Sufi Tradition who are managing its activities worldwide at any one time. Each Qutub is responsible for a given geographical area.

Robe or Kirka : A robe or cloak which is put on before an exercise to help focus the activity, and taken off immediately after. It is never worn publicly. Sufis have been historically associated with the " patched" or " patchwork" robe.

Sheikh : Spiritual Master of the Path, known as " Pir" in Persian, who guides others through the Sufi Tradition. There are two types of Sheikh recognized in Sufism : either the perfected teacher who alone has the authority to teach the Path, or the formalistic teacher who preserves the forms of the Tradition but who does not have the celestial permission needed to initiate the teaching process. The authority of the Sheikh concerns the domain of the Spirit, and a religious authority who deals with the outer observances such as the Ulema or Islamic Jurisprudent can have nothing to say about the inner life.

Shia : The minority sect of Islam that owes its allegiance to its Imams, beginning with the Imam Ali, son-in-law of the Prophet. The Shia claim that he should have been the successor to the Prophet when Muhammed died, that the first three Caliphs were interlopers, and that the Imams should have ruled the Islamic community. Further divisions have split the Shia over time, sometimes into extreme tendencies : the Twelvers of Persia and the Zaydis of Yemen are the most moderate, whereas the Seveners or Ismailis have historically been associated with extremist groups of every kind. Among the Twelvers, for instance, the cult of the 12 Imams (Ali to al-Mahdi) practically effaces the importance of the Prophet Muhammed in the community.

Silsila : The chain of teachers in a Sufi order, connecting the present Master to the Prophet in an unbroken lineage. When evoking the sequence of names in a silsila, one begins with God, then the Archangel Gabriel (Jibril in Arabic) then Muhammad, and so on down to the teachers of the present day. The basic notion of the silsila is the unbroken succession of the teaching as exemplified by and updated through the successive Masters, who alone are authorized to initiate the Bayat or act of commitment. It can be considered that there are two forms of spiritual inheritance deriving from the Prophet Muhammed : on the one hand the world of external religious and ethical observance, and on the other the inner and esoteric spiritual teaching which must remain non-specific in order to provide enough flexibility for each successive teacher to improvise within its framework, thus updating it anew for each generation.

Sunna : The standard body of the words and deeds of the Prophet, as transmitted by his followers and companions, mainly through the collections of hadith or traditions. Generally speaking, the Sunna is considered to be the application of the more general and non-specific material contained in the Koran. The Prophet Muhammed was illiterate, and remained so until his death : this is one of the reasons why his call was first doubted and then be-lieved, because such a book from a known illiterate could only be of Divine origin. In this sense the Koran is consider-ed to be the words of God, whereas the sunna is the words of Muhammed the man, albeit divinely inspired. This material, which was put together in documentary form, goes into precise detail on ritual, political, military, fin-ancial, family, matrimonial, mystical and even sexual questions. The amount of material detail in this body of work is so great that many people have ignored the mystical material in the Sunna, which sometimes contra-dicts the rest of the corpus, and have devoted themselves to an overly meticulous observance right down to minute details, thus leading themselves into spiritual extinction. The multiplicity of forms in the Sunna can therefore disperse the mind and encourage excessive formalism. It nevertheless remains one of the great bodies of knowledge of Mankind.

Sunni : One who belongs to the mainstream of the Moslem community, as opposed to the Shia. Certain sects within the Shia, such as the Twelvers, are close to the Sunni, although even here there are basic political differences due to conflicting ideas about the succession of the Prophet and the cult of the Imams. Sunnis consider that the Shia have distorted Islam by their quasi-deification of Ali, son-in-law of the Prophet, and feel that they themselves uphold the norms of religious and political life as established by the first three Caliphs of Islam, who are rejected by the Shia.

Tarika : A synonym of Sufism. The word means path, in

the spiritual and contemplative sense, as opposed to the word Sharia which is concerned with the life of action. One leaves the Sharia to go towards the Tarika, which involves a change in the scale of one's intention, with the objective of attaining the Al-Hakika or Divine Reality. It's general meaning is " spiritual path" and the word is often used by Sufis to refer to their particular order. Sufis will very often use the word " Tarika" in preference to " Sufism" because they feel that once the Path has become an "ism" it is no longer an organic part of the Sufi Tradition, but an intellectual outcrop of it. For the same reason they will tend to call themselves "seekers" or " friends" rather than " Sufis".

Tasbee : Moslem rosary. Generally made up of 33 stones with a separation after every 11th one. The number of stones correspond to a multiple of the 99 names or Attributes of God.

Tekkia : Meeting-place where group exercises are organized. It can be a place which is specifically built or reserved for this activity, or else a place where other activities take place at other times.

Zikr or Recitation : An exercise which takes the form of a repetition of one of the suhras of the Koran. The sound or cadentic value of these exercises are important, as are their associated breathing rhythms. For this reason they are performed in the original language.

■

SELECTED READING LIST

Omar Ali-Shah : *THE COURSE OF THE SEEKER,* Tale Weaver Publishing, 636 N. Robertson Blvd., Los Angeles, California 90069, U.S.A., 1988, *LE CHEMIN DU CHERCHEUR* (en préparation), ed. Tractus, Paris.

Omar Ali-Shah (trans.) : *THE GARDEN OF ROSES* (GULISTAN) **by Sheikh Saadi of Shiraz** (in preparation) & *LE JARDIN DE ROSES* (GULISTAN) **de SAADI,** Paris, 1988, Editions Albin Michel, 22 rue Huyghens, 75014 Paris.

Robert Graves & Omar Ali-Shah (trans.) : THE RUBAIYYAT OF OMAR KHAYAAM, London 1967, Cassell / Penguin Books, London, 1967.

Rafael Lefort : *THE TEACHERS OF GURDJIEFF* , London, 1977, Gollancz, & *LES MAITRES DE GURDJIEFF* , Editions Le Courrier du Livre, 21 rue de Seine, 75006 Paris

Jalaludin Rumi : *THE MATHNAVI* **(trans. R.A. Nicholson)** Luzac & Co., 46 Great Russell St., London, & *MATHNAWI, LA QUETE DE L'ABSOLU* , Paris 1990, (trad. Eva de Vitray-Meyerovitch & Djamchid Mortazavi) Editions du Rocher, Monaco.

Rumi : *LE LIVRE DU DEDANS / FIHI MA FIHI* **(trad. Eva de Vitray Meyerovitch** , Paris 1975, Editions Sinbad, 1 et 3 rue Feutrier, 75018 Paris.

Rumi : *ODES MYSTIQUES / DIWAN DE SHAMS I TABRIZ* Paris 1973, **(trad. Eva de Vitray-Meyerovitch & Mohammed Mokri),** Editions Klincksieck, 11 rue de Lille, 75007 Paris.

Ernest Scott : *THE PEOPLE OF THE SECRET* , London 1983 The Octagon Press, London, & *LES GARDIENS INVISIBLES* **(trans. Geneviève Mitchell & Ivan Alidjian)** , ed. Le Courrier du Livre, Paris.

Idries Shah : *THE SUFIS* , London 1964, The Octagon Press, P.O. Box 227, London N6 4EW, U.K. & *LES SOUFIS ET L'ESOTERISME* , Paris, 1972, Presses Universitaires de France (épuisé).

Idries Shah : *THE WAY OF THE SUFI* , London 1968
LEARNING HOW TO LEARN , London 1978
Penguin Books, Harmondsworth, Middlesex, U.K.